STRATEGIES
that WIN
SALES

BEST PRACTICES
OF THE WORLD'S LEADING
ORGANIZATIONS

MARK MARONE & SELESTE LUNSFORD
AchieveGlobal

Dearborn™
Trade Publishing
A **Kaplan Professional** Company

Vice President and Publisher: Cynthia A. Zigmund
Acquisitions Editor: Michael Cunningham
Senior Project Editor: Trey Thoelcke
Interior Design: Lucy Jenkins
Cover Design: Jody Billert, Billert Communications
Typesetting: the dotted i

Published by Dearborn Trade Publishing
A Kaplan Professional Company

Printed in the United States of America

05   06   07   10   9   8   7   6   5   4   3   2   1

Library of Congress Cataloging-in-Publication Data
Marone, Mark D.
   Strategies that win sales : best practices of the world's leading organizations / Mark Marone and Seleste Lunsford.
      p.   cm.
   Includes bibliographical references and index.
   ISBN 0-7931-8860-1
   1. Sales management.   2. Selling.   3. Customer relations.
4. Communication in marketing.   I. Lunsford, Seleste E.   II. Title.
HF5438.4.M37 2005
658.8′02—dc22
                                                    2004019868

Dearborn Trade books are available at special quantity discounts to use for sales promotions, employee premiums, or educational purposes. Please call our Special Sales Department to order or for more information at 800-621-9621 ext. 4444, e-mail trade@dearborn.com, or write to Dearborn Trade Publishing, 30 South Wacker Drive, Suite 2500, Chicago, IL 60606-7481.

C o n t e n t s

Today's global economy is moving at such a rapid pace in terms of technology, competition, and changes in market demand that organizations find themselves in the position of having to be more flexible, respond more quickly, and be more creative to remain competitive. The sales organization is in a unique position as it stands at the forefront of meeting and responding to many of the global challenges confronting organizations today. As sales organizations continue to encounter more of everything that makes it difficult to win a sale—more demanding customers, more price pressures, more competition, more channels to market, and the like—they are forced into making important strategic decisions around how they will organize, what technologies they will leverage, and what sales skills they will require.

From an in-depth analysis of 17 of the world's leading organizations, this book explores how major market challenges are being addressed and overcome by the various strategies developed and implemented by sales organizations. Companies in all industries, and particularly their sales organizations, experiment with myriad strategic approaches, from exploring the potential of new sales channels and resegmenting the sales force, to targeting new industries or markets. Through hundreds of hours of interviews, we have identified the following seven primary strategic areas that leading organizations utilize to win sales:

1. Multiple sales channels
2. Sales force segmentation
3. Sales technology

4. Consultative selling
5. Sales force development
6. Sales manager development
7. Sales culture

This book explores in detail each of these strategic areas. For each strategy, we define what it is, we explain the key strategic approach and tactics of it and show why it's important, and, finally, we present the lessons learned and best practices of leading sales organizations. We make no claims that these are the seven most important strategies nor are they the only important ones, but we do believe that doing these well is important for remaining competitive. They are necessary but not sufficient—that is, they're not the only strategies you'll need, but you'd better get these right if you want to consistently win sales.

Following the introduction, the chapters in this book are organized around these seven primary strategies. The introduction first reviews some of the most influential challenges and trends taking place in today's global market, which provides the context and a foundation for the discussion that follows.

Multiple sales channels are the subject of Chapter 2. Here we discuss how sales organizations have developed expanding multichannel strategies that include e-commerce and the development of distributors and alliances in addition to the direct and telesales channels. This chapter explains why and how organizations encourage certain types of customers to buy through a particular channel, and how they treat multichannel customers and customers that are transitioning from one channel to another.

Our second strategy, sales force segmentation, is the topic of Chapter 3. Here we focus on segmentation and deployment of sales resources to meet the challenges of customer demand. This strategy involves aligning the sales force with emerging and evolving customer segments—by account size, volume, and potential, as well as by geography, product type, channel, and the like. This chapter also reviews our findings around formal and informal team selling, and resegmenting of the sales force.

Chapter 4 discusses sales technology strategy as it relates to customer relationship management (CRM) and sales force automation (SFA) system implementations. The chapter focuses on the common pitfalls of CRM/SFA systems, such as resistance to change, past failures, unrealistic vision, ease of use, and not aligning applications with overall strategy, among others. It also reviews critical success factors for implementation and lessons learned from leading sales organizations.

Consultative selling is the topic of Chapter 5. Definitions of consultative selling are presented and we identify when it is and is not appropriate, based on feedback from the organizations that were interviewed. As a concept, consultative selling has been around for well over ten years, yet it hasn't matured in many organizations. These issues are addressed along with such critical success factors as compensation, recruitment, training, and management reinforcement.

Chapter 6 reviews the sales strategy focused on "reskilling" the sales force with the abilities needed to support the other strategies and to function as a differentiator in the marketplace. Reskilling refers to a reevaluation of the sales skills that are required for winning sales in today's business environment. Some skills are new, but even for those that have been around, there is now a higher standard and expectation being applied to them. Furthermore, organizations leverage a strategic approach to resource management to achieve the needed upgrades in the sales force. This involves competency profiling, recruitment, selection, development, retention, and performance management.

Chapter 7 focuses on the important strategy of sales manager development. In the past, organizations have not emphasized training and development of their sales managers. This chapter discusses the implications of not developing managers and, more importantly, the benefits of improving the leadership and coaching abilities of sales managers. In light of internal cost pressures, additional sales channels, and more complex customer segments, organizations are helping managers better manage by looking to technology tools, business processes, and resource development.

The final strategy, developing a sales culture, is discussed in Chapter 8. Culture must be strong and influential and appropriate for the goals, strategies, and business environment of an organization. Rather than merely accepting what they have and possibly fostering bad cultural components, successful sales organizations proactively create, maintain, and evolve their culture. It's all about being flexible and ensuring a fit with the business. This chapter reviews the common pitfalls of sales cultures and lessons learned from successful sales organizations.

In Chapter 9, we present our findings from our survey study of customers. We asked customers how they buy, what drives their decision to buy or not to buy, and what they value in their salesperson and their supplier organization, among other things. What customers really want and what salespeople say customers want may not always align. The important lesson is that for organizations to successfully develop all other strategies discussed in this book, they need to know what their customers value, how they buy, and what leads them to buy—or, more importantly, not to buy. This chapter offers interesting and valuable insights into customers' beliefs, attitudes, and behaviors about buying.

Finally, Chapter 10 draws conclusions regarding the best practices in developing strategies that win sales. As previously mentioned, the strategies discussed in this book aren't the only strategies that sales organizations can pursue to overcome challenges in the marketplace. The ones discussed here, however, were those found to be critical for success for the sales organizations we studied. An overall sales approach that encompasses all of these strategic areas when pursued together represents a comprehensive and systemic approach to winning sales in today's marketplace.

While the findings provided in this book will benefit sales professionals at any level, the lessons learned and best practices regarding each of the strategies are more specifically geared to the sales leaders, strategists, and managers. As you read through each of these chapters, consider what best practices can be applied to your own organization. If you are pursing each of these strategies, what can you do to make them more effective? If you haven't yet developed and implemented all of them, where should you begin? We hope that this book will answer both questions by providing the information you need to make your strategies better and laying a framework for developing those strategies you may be considering.

We would like to express our thanks to those who were instrumental in making this book possible. While this book benefited greatly from the assistance and support of many individuals, we alone assume all responsibility for any errors, omissions, or shortcomings. Ed Del Gaizo conceived the idea to study strategies of successful sales organizations and provided intellectual and moral support during the early stages of the project. Others who provided tremendous help during the interview and data collection process include Katie Clark, Jeanne Schaaf, and Keith Malo. Jeanne, who helped recruit many of the organizations that participated in the study, collaborated with us on the customer survey study that is the subject of Chapter 9. We would also like to thank Bill Jackson and Jerry Keenan for reading parts of the draft and contributing their expertise. Without the support of our managers, Michelle Bonterre and D.L. Karl, this project would have probably lingered much longer than it did. They allowed us to take time away from our other duties without (much) objection to spend time traveling to conduct the interviews and to lock ourselves away to write.

Special thanks go to Jan Birberick for her untiring dedication and assistance in setting up and coordinating interviews, handling correspondences, reading drafts, compiling references, and doing lots of other things while putting up with our often times unclear direction. Finally, we would like to thank the organizations that participated in this study for their time and insight that made this such an immeasurable learning experience. We hope this book returns the favor and provides some valuable insights for other companies interested in developing or improving on their own strategies that win sales.

Our findings about strategies that win sales are based on a year-long study consisting of interviews with more than 150 sales professionals from 16 organizations worldwide and across a variety of industries. We met with sales professionals from all ranks to get a better understanding of their experiences in the field, their observations of their customers' buying attitudes and behaviors, what sales skills they require to be successful, and how their segmentation and sales technology strategies are working. In our study, we first attempted to identify the critical challenges impacting sales organizations, and ultimately, we set out to understand what strategies successful organizations are implementing to address and overcome these challenges.

OUR APPROACH

Organizations were selected to participate based on the performance of their sales organization within their industry. We also looked for companies that had demonstrated success with various strategies involving channel or customer segmentation, training and development of sales skills, or sales technology. Because a sales technology strategy is important for competing in many industries, we focused a portion of our research on organizations that implemented or were in the process of implementing a customer relationship management (CRM) or sales force automation (SFA) system. Other criteria in the selection process were to identify sales organizations that were leading in their respective industries and to find organizations that would provide us a representative sample across industries and geographic regions, including those from Europe, Asia, and North America.

Interviews, each typically about an hour in length, consisted of both face-to-face and telephone conversations. We personally visited all but a few organizations so that we could observe firsthand the sales culture of the organization. On-site visits provided us a richer understanding of the sales operation and allowed us to ask more follow-up and deeply probing questions. We interviewed people at the following levels within each organization:

- Heads of sales who were responsible for strategy development
- Regional sales leaders who were responsible for the implementation of strategies across regions or areas
- Sales managers who were responsible for identifying and developing sales representatives and managing the sales process
- Training professionals who were responsible for developing the skills of the sales force
- Frontline sales representatives who met with customers on a daily basis and were responsible for executing strategies

As part of our investigation we reviewed documents from each company, including organizational charts, strategy statements, training programs, marketing collateral, annual reports, and descriptions of product or service offerings, to gain a better understanding of how each sales organization worked, and where it was experiencing either challenges or successes in each of the seven primary strategic areas.

WHAT WE ASKED

The focus of the study was on how successful organizations responded to changes in the marketplace through strategies centered around sales technology, organizational structure, sales channels, sales management development, new sales skills requirements, and sales culture. Our overarching questions related not only to how marketplace trends impacted a sales organization's ability to compete, but more importantly, what strategies they were developing to win sales in this new environment. More specifically, we investigated the following areas and sought answers to the following questions:

- *Changes in customer behavior.* What is different about customers today compared with five years ago, and what will be different in the future? What challenges do changes in customer behavior present to the sales organization?
- *Adoption and usage of sales technology.* How advanced are the company's use of CRM/SFA systems? What challenges have they posed for the organization? What are the next generation going to look like, and what lessons were learned for future implementations?
- *Sales organization structures.* What channels to market are utilized today and why? What kinds of sales resources are utilized (sales teams, account managers, etc.) and how are they deployed?
- *Selling processes and practices.* What is the common selling approach of each organization participating in the study and how is this similar or different from their competitors? Are selling practices based on any particular philosophy and, if so, what is that philosophy? How might this change in the future?
- *Sales management.* How are managers selected? What are their key responsibilities and skill sets, and how has that

changed over time? How are they trained and prepared in each organization?

- *Sales skills requirements.* What types of sales skills are necessary to achieve the benefits of the strategies being implemented to win sales? Are there new sales skills required and are there old ones that are still valid? Where are the common skill gaps?
- *Sales culture.* What role does the sales culture play in implementing strategies that win sales? What makes for a strong sales culture and what are the challenges to maintaining an influential sales culture?

In addition to our qualitative interviews and analyses of sales organizations, we thought it was important to better understand customer behavior and the challenges it presents to sales organizations by hearing from customers themselves. In a joint study with Schaaf (2004), we surveyed more than 500 customers of information technology from midsized organizations to compare what customers want and value in their salesperson and their buying experience with what sales organizations think customers want and value. This part of our study provides interesting insight into what customers really expect from their vendors and their salesperson and what they say influences their decision to buy or not to buy.

WHO WE INTERVIEWED

The organizations participating in the study all have significant sales organizations that successfully win sales through the design and implementation of one or more of the seven strategies focused on in this book. These top-selling organizations are well known in their industry, and we hope the reader will be able to draw from many of the best practices and lessons learned to leverage in his or her own business. The following is an alphabetical list of organizations that participated in the study, along with a brief description of their business (additional information on each company can be found on their respective Web sites):

- *BellSouth,* based in Atlanta, Georgia, is a Fortune 100 communication services company. The company and its partners serve more than 45 million local, long distance, Internet, and wireless customers throughout the United States and 13 other countries. The company's small business services division, which targets businesses spending $3,000 or less per month on telecommunication services, offers local, long distance, wireless, high-speed Internet access, and multisite fiber connections to small businesses across a 9-state region in the Southeastern United States.

- *Diebold, Inc.,* is a global leader providing integrated self-service delivery systems and services. They develop, manufacture, sell, and service automated financial transaction systems, security equipment, and research and development. The company is one of the leading producers of automated teller machines (ATMs) in the United States. Founded in 1859, Diebold employs more than 13,000 associates with representation in more than 88 countries worldwide and headquarters in Canton, Ohio.

- *Fuji-Xerox* manufactures such products as digital printers, digital copiers, multi-function machines, projectors, engineering plotters, image processing systems, fax machines, and related software. A 50-50 joint venture when it was founded in 1962, Fuji-Xerox is owned by Fuji Photo Film and Xerox.

- *Hewlett Packard (HP)* is a technology solutions provider to consumers, businesses, and institutions globally. The company's offerings span information technology (IT) infrastructure, personal computing and access devices, global services and imaging, and printing for consumers, enterprises, and small and midsized businesses. HP has a team of 142,000 employees with capabilities in 170 countries, and conducts business in more than 40 currencies and more than 10 languages.

- *Honda Clio Shin* develops, manufactures, distributes, and provides financing for the sale of its motorcycles, automobiles, power products, and related parts. A subsidiary of Honda Motor Co., Honda Clio Shin is the largest dealer network in Tokyo, and considered to be one of the best in class Honda car dealers within the Honda Japanese network. Honda Clio Shin employs more than 750 people and concentrates on the luxury market.

- *Infineon Technologies* is a leading innovator in the international semiconductor industry. They design, develop, manufacture, and market a broad range of semiconductors and complete system solutions targeted at selected industries. Their products serve applications in the wireless and wire line communications, automotive, industrial, computer, security, and chip card markets.

- *Infineum* is a joint venture between ExxonMobil Chemical Company, a division of the Exxon Mobil Corporation, The Shell Petroleum Company, and Shell Oil Company. Infineum has more than 70 years of experience in formulating high-quality fuel, lubricant, and specialty additives. Infineum additive technology is underpinned by a worldwide research and development, manufacturing, and supply network.

- *Ingersoll Rand* is a global innovation and solutions provider and features a portfolio of worldwide businesses comprised of leading industrial and commercial brands, such as Bobcat compact equipment, Club Car golf cars, Dresser-Rand turbo machinery, Schlage locks, and Thermo King transport temperature controls, among many others. They employ approximately 45,000 employees worldwide, and operate more than 100 manufacturing facilities, half of which are located outside the United States.

- *Intier Automotive Inc.*, a subsidiary of Magna International, is a Canadian supplier and integrator of automotive interior enclosure components, systems, and modules. Intier Automotive has more than 24,000 employees throughout North America, Brazil, Europe, and Asia Pacific, and 71 production facilities, 17 product development, engineering, and testing centers, and 16 sales offices.

- *Marriott International* is a worldwide operator and franchisor of hotels and related lodging facilities. In the lodging business, which includes the full-service, select-service, extended-stay, and timeshare segments, the company develops, operates, and franchises hotels and corporate housing properties under 14 separate brand names, which encompasses wholly owned direct mail, contract, retail, and Internet operations in 14 countries outside of North America.

- *Office Depot,* a worldwide supplier of office products and services, has three divisions: North American retail division, which markets office products and other business-related services; business services group division, which provides contract office supply; and an international division.

- *Shell Korea,* a part of Shell, Inc., is a global group of energy and petrochemical companies operating in over 145 countries and employing more than 119,000 people. Shell is best known to the public for service stations and for exploring and producing oil and gas on land and at sea, but they deliver a wider range of energy solutions and petrochemicals to customers.

- *Stora Enso* is an integrated paper, packaging, and forest products company producing publication and fine papers, packaging boards, and wood products—areas in which they are a global market leader. Stora Enso has close to 44,000 employees in more than 40 countries spanning 5 continents. Customers are large and small publishers, printing houses, and merchants, as well as the packaging, joinery, and construction industries worldwide.

- *Taishin International Bank,* since its establishment on March 23, 1992, has constantly expanded its scope of business and its operating network, performing the role of an intermediary in the supply and demand of funds for society and providing financial services to promote economic prosperity. The bank's main business includes deposits, loans, bills discounting, remittances, guarantees, short-term bills brokerage and proprietary dealing, import and export negotiation, and foreign-currency deposits.

- *TD Waterhouse,* since 1979, has provided a mix of products, prices, and services that customers need to manage their own investments and personal finances. TD Waterhouse has more than 150 branch offices in major cities throughout the United States. They provide investors with a broad range of brokerage, mutual fund, banking, and consumer financial products and services on an integrated basis.

- *Yellow Book USA,* founded in 1930, is one of the nation's largest publishers of yellow pages directories with more than 500 directories in 42 states and the District of Columbia. Yellow Book also publishes college directories, city and county directories, and a business-to-business directory serving Long Island, New York. The fast-growing company's publications have a circulation of 71 million and an advertiser base of more than 400,000.

Chapter 1 reviews the significant market challenges faced by each of these organizations. Many of you will be quite familiar with these challenges and may be developing strategies of your own to counteract them and the impact they have on winning sales. These are by no means the only important trends or challenges out there, nor are they necessarily the most important ones for every company. They do, however, represent those mentioned most often because they continue to have a significant impact on the ability of the organizations in our study to remain competitive, and they are the key drivers of the strategies reviewed throughout this study.

1

CHALLENGES FACING TODAY'S SALES ORGANIZATIONS

Challenges confronting the modern sales organization cross multiple lines; sometimes they're externally driven, sometimes internally driven, and other times the result of both inside and outside influences. External "macro" challenges include those market forces, such as changes in industry structure, global prices, demand, regulations, and the like, that impact the way organizations sell and conduct business. For example, consolidation in an industry resulting from merger and acquisition activity reduces the number of customers available to suppliers, thus forcing a reassessment of sales strategies. One organization in our study had their customer base reduced from nearly a dozen to just three as a result of mergers and acquisitions. In addition, a decline in global prices may require suppliers to differentiate themselves in new and unique ways. World prices for paper and other forestry products, for example, have been pushed so low that manufacturers now have to create new and innovative value-added services to set them apart from competitors.

Organizations also face external challenges that are derived from changes in the buying behavior of their customers. These more "micro" trends, such as a more demanding and knowledgeable customer base, impact the way sales organizations interact with customers. Because customers are savvier and more knowledgeable about pricing and product features, salespeople need to rethink their approach to selling. Such challenges increase over time as suppliers continue to advance their capabilities (in search of differentiation), which ultimately increases the expectations of customers and encourages competitive response, thus eliminating the differentiation and resulting in the need for a new product or service innovation. It's a never-ending cycle.

Finally, there are those challenges internal to the sales organization that companies must confront, such as internal pressures to reduce costs, turnover, and mergers and acquisitions to name a few. These challenges are not necessarily "bad," and with the right strategy in place they provide organizations with real opportunities for improvement and growth.

Although each organization we interviewed operates in a different industry with individual circumstances (e.g., some were fragmented, some consolidated), all organizations in the study were facing similar challenges with regard to the markets they operated in. These challenges for many were the key drivers in deciding what strategies to pursue and how to operate their sales organizations.

Globalization, mergers and acquisitions, declining prices, and stiffer competition are just a few of the challenges faced by businesses today, and the organizations we studied are no different. Some trends are newer on the scene, such as recent advancements in sales technology, new channels to market including e-commerce, and more knowledgeable customers resulting from information available on the Internet, while others, such as globalization and price pressures, have been around for a while. In response, organizations are pursuing both new and old strategies. This book examines the best practices of sales organizations in developing and implementing these strategies in light of the challenges discussed in the following sections.

GLOBALIZATION

Globalization can refer, from a demand standpoint, to the process of converging preferences across different markets, and simply the availability of more customers to sell to. From a supply perspective, globalization offers opportunities to source the cheapest materials worldwide and to locate production in the most favorable locations. Both of these facets of globalization present challenges and opportunities to organizations, especially those that are becoming more global in scope.

Although the terms are often used interchangeably, a global company and a multinational company are not the same. Multinational indicates that an organization has some presence in more than one country; as opposed to adapting standards or processes to a multitude of local preferences, they're just simply there. For example, a local manufacturer of furniture may sell to regions throughout Asia, but the company is operating as a multinational company and not as a global company. A true global company, on the other hand, has more rigorous requirements as it goes worldwide with the customer, adopting the same standards, languages, networks, and processes for each location, each step of the way. The major global organizations are well known, such as Coca-Cola, but often times they are so global in scope that the location of their headquarters is not apparent.

The globalization of markets and operations represents both challenges and opportunities for sales organizations. While globalization offers bigger markets, along with that comes competition, price pressures, delivery and logistic challenges, local requirements, and cultural adaptation to name a few. According to one company we met with, "Globalization means interpersonal skills must become intercultural skills."

In addition, globalization creates issues for many newly merged organizations as they struggle to leverage their new global capabilities even when products, resources, cultures, and infrastructure are yet to be integrated. These organizations need to represent one face to a global customer, a critical but difficult feat to accomplish. Customer and prospect organizations that have true global reach can be a real challenge for the sales organization.

For many of the organizations we studied, globalization means that their customers have more choices; it means that it may cost more to serve a broader base of customers; it means new competitors on the scene; it means finding and coordinating salespeople across markets; but it also means new revenue opportunities. One company representative commented, "You have to assume a global approach and that means knowing how your big customer's business works in North America, in Europe, *and* in Asia, for example."

Not all organizations we studied are global companies; indeed, some only operate in one or two markets. But all of the organizations are challenged in one way or another by the forces of globalization. Take, for instance, the global transparency of pricing and product resulting from the Internet presence that organizations must have, or the increase of foreign competitors as multinational and global organizations enter home markets. Globalization, rather than being a passing fancy, has only continued to become a more influential and significant factor sales organizations must take into account when developing their strategies.

COMPETITION

For many organizations, competition—both domestic and international—has become more fierce, necessitating explicit strategies for differentiating and remaining competitive. As an outcome of several trends, including globalization, competition grows when organizations become more similar, regardless of how many players there are. Organizations know they are in a seriously competitive environment, whether there is only one other competitor or a thousand competitors, if they cannot differentiate themselves—that is, by adding more value, a different value, or the same value at a lower cost than the other guy(s). According to one company, "The only way to grow is to take something away from a competitor. . . . Today, more people are after less business and we need a bigger piece of a smaller pie."

Today, all players, prospective customers, and true competitors alike have access to much of the same knowledge and many of the same resources. Furthermore, yesterday's competitive differentiators, such as price or securing a presence on the Internet and the ability to deliver via the Web, are no longer unique points of difference. This has leveled the playing field in many industries.

Competition no longer comes only in the form of other organizations that do the same thing and sell to the same markets. Increasingly, organizations are competing against their distributors or agents, against companies providing "substitute" products and services, and internally across their own channels to market in the form of channel conflict. There was no sales organization or salesperson in our study that did not feel competitive pressures on a daily basis. Competition may come in different forms, but identifying competitive sources and managing their impact through the strategies discussed in this book will help organizations to differentiate themselves in the marketplace.

CHANGES IN CUSTOMERS' BUYING BEHAVIORS

Customers aren't necessarily buying different products and services, but they are buying in different ways—by leveraging their knowledge of pricing and product, by expecting more from their vendor and salesperson, and by placing value on different factors that drive decisions to buy. Customers have become more critical and often times less willing to entertain high salesperson involvement. This means that while sales organizations are striving to become consultants to their customers, customers themselves are moving toward reverse auctions, procurement committees, and other arm's-length buying models that make it more challenging for the salesperson to add value, and resulting in a need for new sales approaches.

Every organization we spoke with reported some degree of change in their primary purchasers' behaviors and attitudes. Those shifts represented a range of themes from increased expectations of their vendors and salespeople to an exclusive focus on price. In Chapter 9 we discuss in more detail how customers have changed the way they buy and what they value, and present data from our own examination of buying behaviors from the customers' points of view.

Across the globe, customers and prospects expect faster delivery of higher-quality products and services with far less tolerance for a misstep or error—yet all for less money. Customers are more sophisticated today and their demands are escalating with no apparent end in sight. Sales organizations are having to continuously reinvent themselves to keep up, and are constantly pressured to provide more at a lower price. Customers have also grown intensely price focused, even at the expense of their relationship with their salesperson. To that end, customers and prospective customers have abandoned the conversation on features, benefits, and value and have redirected attention toward gaining an immediate price concession. According to one manager, "Requests for price reductions are relentless, just relentless." Further complicating matters, some customers have become accustomed to receiving lower price points, which may have been provided out of desperation during tough times "to secure the business." Now, any attempt to increase price leads customers to look at competitive alternatives.

Finally, the growing phenomenon of reverse auctions is putting the customer in the driver's seat in terms of dictating product, delivery, price, and terms. In a reverse auction, a buyer will send an electronic proposal of sorts stipulating the specifications and the delivery of the products they wish to buy. Vendors then log on to the auction to submit their bids with the lowest price generally winning (see Chapter 9 for a more in-depth discussion of electronic auctions). Buyers typically make no guarantees to buy and suppliers are left to a bidding war. As one sales manager told us, "I have nightmares over these reverse auctions."

Customers are also "commoditizing" products and services or reducing products and services to discrete units, be it ATM machines, paper, or hotel rooms. This is occurring in many of the industries we studied despite the type of product or service offering. Therefore, understanding the customer's business and building professional relationships are more critical than ever but, at the same time, even harder to achieve. While salespeople commonly want to be a strategic or trusted business advisor to their customers, purchasers have a tendency to see the salesperson's product or service as merely "another good." This arm's-length or more hands-off approach to the sales process by the customer is presenting clear challenges to contemporary sales techniques and tactics.

There's no doubt that customer satisfaction is important, and as the old adages go, the customer is always right, the customer comes first, etc. But giving away the store won't necessarily result in satisfied and loyal customers. One manager told us, "If you want loyalty, buy a dog. You won't get loyalty from customers." Probably a bit cynical, but not far from the truth, especially when sales organizations don't have customer strategies in place. Successful sales organizations know that meeting and exceeding the expectations of customers and providing the value they are shopping for requires smart strategies that will involve sales skills, technology, and a culture of service among other things. Top organizations also know that always meeting the demands of customers, regardless of what those demands are, can be detrimental to both parties. Taking this into account, knowing when to bend over backward and when to say no when developing sales-related strategies is essential.

COMPLEX SALES CYCLES

Changes in the way customers buy also have increased the complexity and the length of the sales cycle even in what are traditionally transactional markets. Buyers are more cautious in making investments and there are more choices, which often lead to longer buying decision processes. In addition, many consumers now rationalize their buying decisions by taking cues from peers, seeking advice, and conducting their own research to get the best product at the best price. Consumers and business buyers are now logging on to the Internet more frequently for information on products and pricing. Rather than a consumer buying something in the store, they may go home and spend days, if not weeks, searching for a better deal—or even the same deal without paying taxes and shipping.

Sales cycles become lengthier and more complex as salespeople have to deal with third parties, such as purchasing committees and procurement professionals, only concerned with hammering out the lowest price. One manager noted, "Procurement has ten times the power than they did four to five years ago." Finally, this trend in lengthy and complex sales cycles is also a result of sales organizations trying to elevate their presence and participation in the sales process by identifying and solving business issues.

The buyers and purchasing processes of yesterday are no longer the purchasers and practices of today. To a great extent, this shift can be taxing for both sales professionals and their sales organization in terms of the energy and resources they consume. Further challenging the sales organization is the fact that some of these challenges require new skill sets that require investments in training. The sales professionals we interviewed most notably observed increased investment in the sales cycle via:

- A more formal request for proposal (RFP), even from long-term and existing customers
- The presence of purchasing committees of varying shapes, sizes, and scopes
- The increasing power of procurement departments
- Stricter requirements to demonstrate a real return on investment (ROI), providing proof of their organization's financial solvency, and more on-site demonstrations
- The number of senior leaders involved with purchasing decisions replacing a lower ranking associate who would have previously made the purchasing decision independently
- Longer sales cycles, making it harder to get a commitment from customers
- The presence of third parties, such as external consultants and procurement departments, selecting vendors and making buying decisions
- Increased centralized or corporate-based buying as purchasing authority has been stripped of field offices

These trends have resulted in longer sales cycles in addition to making sales processes more difficult and more resource intensive for the salesperson. With more players to deal with, additional decision layers to negotiate, and standardized requirements that mean more work for the salesperson, making a sale has become an increasingly complex activity.

HEIGHTENED PERFORMANCE
EXPECTATIONS

Being on the front line, the salesperson directly confronts many of these challenges on a daily basis. Consequently, organizations require that their sales professionals possess the necessary skills for overcoming these challenges and winning sales. Sales professionals at all levels identified a number of human resource concerns that have a real impact on the sales organization's success. As marketplaces mature and evolve, some of the skill sets required of yesterday's successful sales professionals have likewise changed. For example, learning how to sell to new audiences, such as senior business leaders and more savvy consumers, being trained to effectively link the benefits of a product offering to a prospect's bottom line or an individual's hidden personal needs, or understanding how to interpret financial statements to determine profitable versus unprofitable opportunities are critical skills for winning sales. Yet once again, these emerging training needs arise at a time marked with tighter training budgets.

We interviewed some organizations, especially in the technology sector, that participate in markets that require salespeople to possess some degree of technical knowledge. Lack of technical competence in some industries can put the salesperson at a disadvantage, especially in the absence of a cross-functional team-selling environment. Moreover, finding and keeping salespeople with a mix of sales experience and the necessary technical aptitude can be a daunting assignment. Technological competence is also important from the standpoint of being able to fully leverage the sales technologies, such as a customer relationship management (CRM) or sales force automation (SFA) system, that organizations today rely on.

Like most company divisions, the sales organization wrestles with recruiting, hiring, developing, and retaining individuals who have strong skill sets and a good cultural fit. Many sales

managers pointed out that it is all about hiring the right people from the start, and then training them to achieve their
potential. Once the talent is onboard, it's critical that the organization be focused on developing and improving the necessary skill sets of its people. Striking and sustaining a perfectly
balanced sales force—recruiting right and training right—to
maintain competitive advantage, under any circumstance, is no
small feat.

Other sales managers also shared that "working with what
we've got" was a significant obstacle to their success. In response,
some forward-thinking sales organizations avoid the hazards of
complacency by continuously reassessing sales responsibilities,
positions, and individual strengths to maximize resources for
the best gains.

Sales skills and professional development among sales managers is equally as important but has received far less attention
in many organizations. So often, sales managers achieve their
role based on sales expertise and have little or no leadership
skills, which can hamper their ability to successfully navigate the
daily maze of hurdles and to keep focused on the bigger picture. The lack of time, resources, and support for training managers further inhibits sales leadership development, and, when
all combined, can present the sales organization with some significant challenges—starting at the higher levels.

INTERNAL RESOURCES CONSTRAINTS

Once again, just as customers and prospects have been
charged with minimizing costs to maximize profit, so too has the
sales organization. Downsizing, cost cutting, increasing span of
control, and expecting more output with fewer resources are
just a sampling of the internal challenges echoed by the organizations we studied. Said one manager, "A 15 percent market
downturn causes us to lay off 20 percent of our staff." Another

told us that "now I have 20 direct reports as a result of reorganizing and it's getting hard to have direct contact with each." Other internal performance and cost hurdles impacting sales organizations, not only in our study but across many industries, include:

- The "raising of the bar," as there is greater demand that salespeople acquire profitable business with revenue quotas increasing every year
- Increasing overall revenues expected as the size of the sales force decreases
- Bigger territories resulting from downsizing the sales organization
- Reduction of support staff as a means of lessening the organization's payroll, thus placing more administrative duties in the hands of salespeople who need to be on the street
- Cutbacks in incentives and recognition programs partly to minimize expenses and achieve higher margins but also to reward only top-tier performers
- Sales staff turnover, both voluntary and involuntary
- Increased span of control, whereby managers must lead much larger teams than in the past

These internal challenges place considerable pressure on everyday sales activities and can impact the ability of the salesperson to execute strategies in the field. In fact, these challenges impact the performance of strategies in other areas, including the adoption of sales technologies, segmenting the sales force, and creating a strong and influential sales culture. While the organizations we interviewed were experiencing internal cutbacks and cost constraints to varying degrees, all seemed to be negatively affected in one way or another compared to the more favorable business environment of the late 1990s.

OVERCOMING CHALLENGES WITH STRATEGIES THAT WIN SALES

We emphasize the significance of these challenges because they are internal and external factors that precipitate change and action in the corporation. Sales organizations are particularly vulnerable to many of these challenges and as such address them through various strategic plans. These challenges are real issues for many organizations beyond just those that participated in our study. Other research demonstrates the widespread impact that these issues have on organizations across industries and regions. For example, a recent study of 1,300 sales executives (Dickie and Trailer, 2004) found the following:

- Sales executives reported that their top three business objectives for the year were: increase revenues, increase sales effectiveness, and increase market share.
- On average, just less than half of their sales representatives were able to meet or exceed their quota for the past year—the lowest level since the survey was first conducted ten years ago.
- One-third believed that the administrative burden on sales representatives is increasing.
- More than half, or 54 percent, reported that forecasted sales are lost to competitors or to no decision.
- Fifty-three percent reported they had implemented a CRM system, yet only 26 percent of those same organizations said they were achieving significant improvements in performance.
- More than half, or 58 percent, surveyed said they do not have a formal selling methodology.

While this book explores a number of strategies to successfully meet many of the challenges reviewed in this chapter, the central theme is that for the contemporary sales organization to be successful in the face of more—more demand, more competition, more customer expectations—it has to be flexible with all its processes, structures, and resources, including human and technological. An effective and winning sales organization is one that is able and willing to be flexible, to reinvent itself, and to redeploy resources accordingly. It also has to have the right strategies in place—those strategies that will create sales opportunities out of business challenges in the marketplace.

As any successful sales professional knows, organizations don't generally grow by sitting on the sidelines or by staying immersed in yesterday's crises. Organizations grow by always looking forward. We interviewed a number of organizations that constantly look ahead and have developed adaptable sales strategies to meet changing needs. We hope you will find some of their stories viable for your own sales organization.

New opportunities are out there—even in the face of all of these challenges. Organizations are trying to figure out how to proactively identify and pursue these opportunities. While at present the common operating model seems to be more reactive, the need for a more strategic approach to business development is a critical requirement for winning sales.

EXPANDING
MULTICHANNEL STRATEGIES

"We need to drive the business to the organization regardless of the channel, and if you do this, it's a win regardless of what channel the sale comes through. We need to let people know that driving business to the company is number one."

—Vice President, Sales

Channels are the means by which selling organizations reach their marketplace. They are used as a bridge between product and service offerings and segments of customers. Almost all of the organizations we spoke with utilized a multichannel strategy and were in the process of adding even more channels to their mix to present the customer with greater options, while in many cases reducing the cost of sale. It is a tricky equation with considerable investment required in creating the processes and infrastructure to support these channels from a personnel and technological perspective. If developed correctly from the start and managed properly on an ongoing basis, multichannel strategies can bring high returns to an organization. If not well designed and governed, adding channels can reduce sales, cannibalize revenue from other channels, and produce counterproductive conflicts among sales resources.

Momentum to Change

There are many drivers behind the need to create (or add to) a multichannel strategy. Some are internally focused, such as a need to reduce the cost of sale, while others are in response to external factors, such as a need to meet a customer expectation. The key to creating a structure that meets all of these needs is to first look at the overall sales strategy. A sales strategy will answer the following four questions:

1. *Who are we?* An organization's brand identity and value proposition will help determine how it wants to manage customer relationships.
2. *What do we sell?* The product or service being sold will impact the appropriateness of channel (e.g., organizations with highly technical products will require live support through distributors or in-house sales representatives, whereas those who sell less complex product sets may benefit from self-service channels).
3. *Who do we sell to?* Channels can be used to meet a variety of customer needs and provide mechanisms to efficiently serve customers of differing potential and preferences. Many will be targeted at specific customers and segments while others will favor a mass-market audience.
4. *How do we sell?* The manner in which relationships with customers are created and managed will help determine what kinds of sales resources are required and how narrow or broad their account responsibilities.

When these four questions are answered and communicated across the sales organization, decisions on channels, as well as resource deployment, skill development, and many of the other strategies addressed in this book, can be made with greater confidence.

DEVELOPING A CHANNEL STRATEGY

Historically, organizations approached channel additions as a way to conduct sales at lower costs. With the advent of e-commerce in particular, it became feasible that lower potential customers could be rendered more profitable by selling to them and serving them through lower cost channels. What happened, however, was that customers did not shift channel usage from a higher cost channel to a lower cost channel. Instead, they used all channels to meet a variety of needs. As a result, organizations were not always able to reduce infrastructure expense—they frequently had to increase it to provide seamless processes across multiple channels.

Take the banking industry, for example. When automated teller machines (ATMs) came to the forefront and Web banking became more commonplace, people were convinced it would mean the death of the bank branch. Instead, the branch has continued to be a core focus for bank customers—only now bank customers use the branch in addition to ATMs, in addition to call centers, in addition to Web banking, depending on their individual needs at the time. Today, customers expect that they will be able to initiate a loan application online and finish it in the branch. They expect that they can receive a bank balance from any channel and have it be calculated the same way. This is a tall order requiring significant investments in customer relationship management (CRM) software and systems integration. It is important to note that not only did channel usage expand rather than shift, bank branches did not die. In fact, banks are now reinvesting in their branches, increasing functionality and overhauling design to meet higher customer expectations for delivery.

The benefits of multichannel strategies have not always been lower cost of sales then, but more likely may reside in the increased revenues from building a better customer experience using the right mix of integrated channel options. Selecting this mix and building the infrastructure to support it can be challenging. Every channel has its own set of strengths and weaknesses, and every addition increases the complexity of an integrated back office. For example, while maintaining a direct sales force provides high personal touch with customers and prospects, it is, however, quite costly. On the other hand, while an Internet site with the ability to accept and process orders is significantly cheaper for an organization to support, it may inhibit the organization's ability to establish personal rapport with its customers.

In our study, we concentrated on channels that were being managed by the sales organization. This is not intended to be a complete discussion of the universe of channel options available to organizations, but is instead a look at how some sales organizations are integrating key channels into a multichannel delivery strategy. Some of the channels discussed within this study include the following:

- *Field sales force.* Face-to-face sales professionals who build and maintain customer relationships
- *Inside sales force.* Telephone-based sales professionals who function similarly to face-to-face sales representatives but conduct business over the telephone instead of in person
- *Telemarketing groups.* Outbound telesales professionals who may or may not be employees and are typically assigned to transactional sales or prospecting activities
- *Indirect sales force.* Third parties, such as distributors, resellers, retailers, and agents, used to reach end customers and increase market coverage
- *E-commerce.* System that allows customers to guide their own buying experience using the Web
- *Inbound call centers.* Centers staffed by service representatives tasked to up-sell or cross-sell customers who call in with service requests

The Field Sales Force

A face-to-face sales force is often considered most appropriate for building deeper, more consultative relationships with customers—effectively acting as a consultant to buyers and functioning as a differentiator in the purchase decision. At the same time, a field sales force represents the highest cost of sale for an organization. Therefore, much work is done to ensure that it operates as efficiently and effectively as possible. (See Chapter 3 for more on how direct sales resources are deployed.)

Despite its expense, however, the face-to-face sales force is in no danger of extinction. As one sales manager noted, "Face-to-face will always have more intimacy. Customers will always tend to cut it short when you are on the phone." So, much like the bank branch, face-to-face selling is here to stay—a core delivery mechanism for many if not most sales organizations. However, to earn an appropriate return on the investment required, many organizations are narrowing the focus of the direct sales force (face-to-face sales resources in particular) to handling purchases of large customers and use other resources, such as inside salespeople, to address smaller customers, and even pre- and postpurchase activities for larger customers. For example, one organization noted, "We are going to improve efficiencies of inside sales to free up higher-end resources. By finding money in the inside sales model, we can invest more in large-account management. By offloading postsale activity and servicing to lower-cost resources, we can devote higher-cost resources to business acquisition."

Another way by which sales organizations utilized face-to-face sales was through a proprietary retail chain. In some cases, a network of locally deployed branches was staffed with sales personnel to handle largely inbound sales traffic. This is used as a mass-market supplement to more targeted channels. Retail sales were not specifically addressed in our study. It is important to note, however, that a retail capability was often used in combination with a field sales force to reach additional market segments. For example, a field sales force was used to sell large quantities or highly customized services to business clients and the retail chain was used for selling small quantities of standardized product to consumers on a more transactional basis. Additionally, some organizations included the retail branch network as an integrated option for both business and consumer clients.

The Inside Sales Teams

In addition to face-to-face resources, most organizations include an inside sales force as part of their direct sales team. The organizations interviewed often described inside sales profes-

Integrating the Field Sales Force, Retail Branches, and E-commerce at Office Depot

Office Depot's Business Services Group (BSG) is responsible for selling and servicing all business accounts across the United States. The BSG's primary means of sale to the marketplace is a direct sales force. However, the company has been successful at leveraging all of its channels—retail stores and the Internet, for example—to the benefit of the BSG and its customers. While customers are typically acquired through a field or inside sales team, they can maintain their account and conduct ordering via the Web channel. Further, if a BSG warehouse is unable to meet a business customer's needs, by using a specifically designed card the customer may visit any retail store to procure their needed item. In doing so, the customer is able to retain their BSG pricing structure and the BSG account manager will receive bonus credit for that in-store purchase. Likewise, if a retail store finds itself unable to meet a visiting business customer's needs, the store will refer the customer to a BSG sales representative for follow-up. In this way, Office Depot customers are able to fully benefit from the variety of channel capabilities.

sionals as "face-to-face sales reps who do everything over the phone." Inside sales professionals were usually aligned with lower potential customers and prospects more often than face-to-face resources were. They are, however, still capable of, and often charged with, forming long-term relationships with clients and handling multicall sales processes, when it's appropriate.

Additionally, many organizations paired inside sales teams with face-to-face sales professionals either to work on different parts of a sales process (inside sales representative prospects and qualifies the account, the field representative makes acquisition sales call, and the inside representative manages the on-going account maintenance) or to handle large accounts (field salesperson calls on headquarters, inside salesperson handles smaller business units). As one organization explained, "We are piloting a team-selling approach between field reps and telesales personnel. We are trying to define handoffs in both directions, see where the lines of demarcation should be, and find out how different kinds of customers want to be handled."

As an inside sales force utilizes many of the same processes as their face-to-face colleagues, some organizations are using this resource as a training ground for field representatives.

Inside Sales versus Telemarketing

Although "inside sales" and "telemarketing" are terms frequently used interchangeably, they have become two very distinct job profiles in practice within the organizations in our study. Telemarketing resources were geared toward selling products and services on a highly transactional basis and typically had one-call sales cycles. Such resources also may be used for prospecting activities, generating and qualifying leads that are passed off to other channels. Telemarketing resources can be internal to the selling organization or can be contracted on an outsource basis.

Although this can be an effective channel for handling very large volumes of transactional activity, its use for business-to-consumer (B2C) transactions in the United States is in flux because recent "Do Not Call" legislation curtails telemarketing use to contact only those consumers who have a current business relationship with a seller or those who have given express permission to be contacted. Thus, B2C telemarketing activity has moved, in the United States, from new customer acquisition to being a cross-sell, up-sell vehicle for existing customers.

Third Parties and Indirect Channels

Many organizations in our study are utilizing third parties to reach their customers. Such organizations can include distributors, outside sales agents, retailers, resellers, wholesalers, dealerships, and more. Third-party organizations are used in a variety of ways to extend the sales coverage of a selling organization, such as the following:

- Distributors and resellers sell, and often repackage, products for specific customer segments, either as discrete offerings or bundled or integrated with other items. These are sometimes sold with the seller's brand, sometimes with the distributor's brand.
- Outside sales agents are usually considered contracted sales resources who represent the selling organization (and in some cases other organizations) to customers located too remote for field coverage.
- Retailers are often resellers of product to individual consumers and small businesses through retail outlets. Typically, in this case, the product is packaged and branded by the selling organization.

Regardless of the type of arrangement, each of these third parties is utilized to bridge the selling organization with end users. Use of these relationships varied by organization. In some cases, the organization was working to eliminate this function and bring more of the sales responsibility in-house. In other cases, the organization was focused on utilizing these relationships to an even greater extent to replace in-house selling resources. While such partnerships can be a tremendous asset toward cost-effectively gaining greater market coverage and presence, they also can reduce control over the brand experience and ultimately inhibit an organization's goal for creating intimacy with its end users. This can be a challenge should channels be restructured and distributors dropped. In fact, a

Partnering with Distributors at Stora Enso

Stora Enso is an integrated paper, packaging, and forest products company producing publication and fine papers, packaging boards, and wood products. To reach its end customers, the company uses both a direct and an indirect channel to market.

The indirect channel is comprised of a select set of key merchants or paper distributors, who then sell to small and medium-sized organizations. Stora Enso's strategy is to work with only a small group of carefully selected merchants who cannot only deliver their product but also "the right kind of experience" to end customers. Some of these are independent organizations. Some are actually owned by competitors. In all cases, Stora Enso views its relationships with these merchants as long-term partnerships. As such, the company is in constant contact with its merchants, providing training and sales support. At times, the end customers of this merchant network wish to deal with Stora Enso directly. Because this can cause channel conflict, Stora Enso has put a structure in place to manage these situations to help the end customer address their needs while at the same time preserving a good working relationship with the merchant. By strategically selecting, developing, and managing these indirect sales resources, Stora Enso is able to complement, rather than compete with, its direct sales force.

recent study (Abele, et al, 2003) indicated that "when a manufacturer drops a distributor . . . 20 to 50 percent of the volume the manufacturer used to enjoy in that territory stays with the distributor."

Although a way to cost-effectively expand coverage, organizations should not underestimate the resources required to manage indirect sales resources. Once the decision is made to leverage these kinds of relationships, the selling organization will often need to support its partners with product knowledge training, marketing materials, industry information, and even sales or management skills training. Furthermore, these relationships frequently require a sales resource to manage them. For many organizations, this is a new role—requiring an individual who not only understands the sales function but who also has the business acumen (e.g., category management skills, marketing insight, and financial expertise) to assist the third party in running their business successfully.

Finally, it should be noted that the organizations studied were continually broadening the scope of the kinds of organizations that they were partnering with. In fact, several used competitors as distribution partners. Intier Automotive, for example, sells components to third parties who then integrate them into their solutions. Some of these third parties are actually direct competitors for other components of Intier Automotive's business.

Technology-Enabled Self-Service

Another channel that has been growing in importance over time is Web-enabled self-service. This channel may work particularly well in situations where the product set is straightforward, and customers have experience with purchasing the product and prefer transactional relationships. Such customers do not always value the input of sales professionals and feel like they can manage all aspects of the buying decision on their own.

From a seller's perspective, this channel can be useful as a means to profitably engage customers who may represent low potential, but it also can represent barriers to building deeper relationships with high-value customers. Therefore, to support their overall organizational goals, organizations we interviewed were migrating to structures where the self-service channel was an integrated part of a multichannel delivery strategy and not a separate business unit.

Organizations tended to use a Web-based channel for the acquisition of self-service customers as well as for account maintenance activity for customers acquired through other channels. For example, one organization uses a direct sales force to acquire new business; however, once committed, the organization trains and strongly encourages its new customers to use the Internet for ordering and account management functions. While operationally cost-effective to have its consumers self-manage their orders, invoices, and utilization reports, if the sales representative keeps too far a distance, this could be damaging to renewal efforts. Therefore, additional focus is placed on in-person, annual account reviews.

Another challenge presented by adding electronic channels into a multichannel structure was a lack of technical integration. As the 1990s progressed, many industries found that an e-commerce presence was a competitive must have. At the same time, they knew that it was a new business model that required a new infrastructure and new technologies (and sometimes a new mind-set). Therefore, to reduce time-to-market, e-commerce channels were often built as silos and were not integrated well with other channels to market. As a result, many organizations still struggle to support transactions across multiple channels (e.g., start a mortgage application online and finish it in the branch) or build a complete view of a customer across the various channels. In fact, a recent study (Compton, 2004) showed that less than 60 percent of financial institutions surveyed were able to communicate a complete view of the customer across the organization. From a customer perspective, this could mean that when you call a banking call center, you may not be able to get access to your mortgage account without being forwarded to another operator. It may also mean that when you get your checking balance from an ATM receipt, it may be different than if you had gotten it from a branch teller.

Many of the organizations we spoke to were in the process of improving their e-commerce capabilities. New directions include functionality to support customers using a blended approach, meaning that customers are not completely self-service but instead can choose to use the Internet for only some aspects of their relationship (what TD Waterhouse calls "clicks and bricks"). In this case, better coordination and integration among channels is needed. Other improvements involve better utilizing the unique strengths of an electronic medium. Just moving a transaction from one channel to another will result in less effective interactions. For example, let's say customers currently use face-to-face sales resources to experience product demos. You could move that very same transaction to the Web by recording a video of a salesperson giving a demonstration. This, however, may be a very flat interaction and leverages none of the qualities that make electronic interaction unique. Instead, you could design a virtual demo whereby customers could guide themselves through simulations to configure and experience custom solutions. In similar fashion, many organizations are looking to provide this kind of sophisticated capability via their online channels.

Leveraging Nonsales Resources

Many organizations utilize nonsales resources to bolster sales activity. As many organizations in our study echoed, "Everyone is in sales; not just salespeople." These can include implementation staff or servicing professionals—anyone who has contact

One Strategy, Multiple Channels at Marriott International

Marriott's philosophy is to sell to people as they want to buy. As such, customers have a variety of choices, including a direct sales force (locally and internationally deployed), regional reservation centers, electronic reservation systems, a proprietary Web site, and other electronic marketplaces, through which they can do business. The company's goal is to "win in every channel" in which they participate. Therefore, the focus is to dominate the market in each channel, switching customers from competitors, rather than trying to shift customers from one Marriott channel to another. Toward that end, Marriott has adopted a pricing strategy such that pricing is consistent regardless of the channel. Under this model, customers are able to more conveniently utilize the channel of their preference instead of chasing deals across channels.

As a result, Marriott does not drive traffic to its Web site using special discounts for online bookings. Instead, Marriott focuses its electronic channel strategy on careful management of its listing in reservation systems and electronic marketplaces, as well as through constant upgrades and detailed monitoring of the use of the Marriott.com Web site to better serve customers who prefer those channels. This has been a beneficial strategy and the Marriott.com Web business continues to grow (with a record year in 2003).

with the customer. As a major focus of many organizations is to deepen relationships with current customers, inbound call centers can be a valuable selling resource. Such centers are staffed with customer service agents and are increasingly asked to cross-sell customers who are calling in for service transactions. This can be an effective strategy, though it also presents its own set of challenges in implementation. The biggest issue is that the service personnel often are not comfortable with the idea of selling and can be very resistant to it. Additionally, compensation and performance evaluation can be barriers. Many times customer service agents are evaluated by their ability to resolve customer issues quickly. So it can be confusing as a service representative to be instructed to try to get a customer off the phone as quickly as possible and at the same time cross-sell them. This confusion can be very damaging.

Research into the effectiveness of service-to-sales activity at call centers (Aksin, 1999) has found that without proper implementation, refocusing customer service resources on sales efforts can decrease service levels. Therefore, to reap the benefits without suffering lower service quality, particular attention should be paid to commitment building, training, system functionality, and process design. Marriott International, for example, helps their reservations personnel understand that their focus is solely on maximizing the value of every call. Therefore, they do not focus on agent talk time but instead emphasize getting the value out of each customer interaction. The result: They have successfully created a highly leveraged, world-class call center network that boasts "a Triple Crown of lowest cost, highest conversion, and highest contribution to filling hotels."

MANAGING CHANNEL CONFLICT

As more and more channels are being introduced into the marketplace, conflict among those channels becomes inevitable. This can happen when multiple sales resources target the same account. For example, an inside sales representative and international account manager both engage with a client because it is not clear who owns the account. As one salesperson admitted, "If you contact three different channels, you will get three different quotes." It also can happen when a customer is assigned to one channel but chooses to interact with a channel other than the one assigned to their account. As an example, a customer may engage a local distributor to buy a product rather than call their business account representative because they need it quickly. If contingencies are not in place to handle these occurrences, inefficiencies for both the buyer and the seller can result.

To prevent situations where multiple sales resources are reaching out to the same customers and creating redundancy, customers (or customer segments) can be assigned to specific sales channels or resources. To do this appropriately requires a strategic approach to market planning, differentiating customers and segments by preferences, behaviors, needs, and, ultimately, potential to the organization. Further, these decisions need to be clearly communicated to sales channels. No salesperson wants to waste time prospecting an account for which there will be no reward. Therefore, setting clear guidelines for which resource owns each account or customer segment can reduce the likelihood that two different sales resources will target the same customer or segment.

Although this can help in the case of seller-initiated communications, there is still the issue of ongoing relationship management and instances where the customer can initiate channel conflict. This can even be intentional, as one sales representative noted, "Sure conflict exists, it's just the nature of the business. Sometimes customers will often stir it up [between manufacturer sellers, brokers, and distributors] just to make sure they are getting the best deal."

Customers will need to be in control of many aspects of the relationship and will need to engage the selling organization to meet their needs. Some organizations have left the choice of what channel to use for these interactions up to the customer. For example, consumers wishing to book rooms with Marriott may do so with their travel agent, in an electronic marketplace, or with a reservations center—any way they wish. In other cases, it may make more sense for a customer to be primarily engaged with a specific channel (e.g., HP assigns dedicated account teams to large corporate accounts). Therefore, customers would engage those resources to manage all the aspects of their relationship because a dedicated team will be closer to the account and will be staffed specifically to support them.

Even when customers or customer segments are carefully assigned to specific channels, however, they are often reluctant to confine channel usage in all cases. A good illustration once again can be found in the banking industry (financial services institutions were at the forefront of multichannel delivery and much can be learned from their early experiences). With the advent of Web banking, some banks created Web-only accounts whereby customers were afforded unlimited ATM use and Web banking for a very low monthly fee. Any use of tellers, however, resulted in high per-transaction fees. The strategy backfired for many institutions as customers originally shifted their activity

Supporting Customer Preference at Taishin International Bank

Founded in 1992, Taishin International Bank provides general commercial banking services through a wide variety of channels to market that permit customers to interact with them according to their preferences.

The bank has a direct sales channel that sells via a face-to-face sales force, telephone banking, branches, and Internet banking. Sales representatives engage with clients using a variety of methods. Importantly, Taishin has created an integrated multichannel delivery system and is able to support interactions that cross channel boundaries, such as face-to-face meeting at a retail establishment followed by fulfillment at a branch or processing on the bank's Web site. Additionally, the bank utilizes an indirect channel including alliance partners, such as real estate agents, mortgage brokers, construction companies, and notaries, as well as third-party marketing firms. In this manner, customers have a choice of how to engage with the bank and are able to not only utilize different channels for different transactions but to also complete the same transaction using different channels.

but then wanted to use the branch for select transactions. The press characterized the branch fees as punishment and fear was fueled that banks would close branches and force customers to use electronic channels. Banks quickly realized that even customers who self-selected for single-channel usage did not want their options restricted.

The reality is that even with the best-laid account assignments there will be cases where a customer might prefer to engage an organization through a variety of channels. There also will be times when account assignments enter gray areas and multiple resources sell into the same account. Therefore, organizations should have processes in place to address these events. Sometimes an organization may be able to reroute a transaction (e.g., if a business customer contacts an inbound call center, they might be able to be forwarded directly to their account rep). Other times, the organization may be able to support the transaction using an integrated data system (as in the Office Depot example where a business customer can use a card to access their account pricing in a retail branch). In other cases where this is not possible, it is usually the sales manager who is called on to mediate disputes (usually regarding revenue recognition and transaction expense).

As such, sales managers will negotiate between business units, or other organizations, to arrive at an outcome that benefits all parties and is seamless to the customer. Because this kind of negotiation can occur across different entities with different business models, it can be challenging as well as time-consuming. Furthermore, as Mehta (2000) and other researchers have noted, this responsibility comes in addition to the other coaching and management duties of the sales manager. (For more information on the increasing complexity of sales management, see Chapter 7.)

To assist managers in this activity, many organizations in our study had established guidelines to determine how to resolve conflict. Increasingly, we noticed that organizations were more willing to engage in "double-counting." This means that credit for sales activity may be awarded to two different channels. For instance, referring back to the Office Depot example, if a business utilizes a retail store, the account rep gets credit for the sale and the store counts the sale toward location revenues. Similarly, at Marriott, if a local hotel does business with a global alliance account, that business is counted toward the revenue goals of the local hotel as well as the account goals of the alliance account manager. Because compensation can be one of the most contentious issues in a sales organization, this double-counting philosophy eliminates the majority of channel conflict issues. Furthermore, it supports a holistic view that the selling organization's goal is to engage customers regardless of channel.

Finally, it should be noted that even though it can damage productivity, some level of channel conflict is not only inevitable, it's desirable. Remember that the idea behind using multiple channels to market is that they can vastly increase an organization's sales footprint and access to a variety of customer segments that could not be efficiently served by a sole field channel. Therefore, a lack of channel conflict can mean that there is not adequate coverage of the prospect universe. As one sales manager noted in our study, "Channel conflict in itself is not bad as long as you can manage it. If you did not have it, it would be because there is not enough activity."

BEST PRACTICES AND LESSONS LEARNED

Not only do customers wish to utilize a variety of channels within the buyer-seller relationship, they frequently use multiple channels to complete even a single, specific transaction. A frequently cited example of this may be found within the airline industry. Customers may contact an airline customer care center or consult with a travel agent for trip planning counsel, hence consuming valuable time and resources, only to turn around and purchase the actual ticket from the lowest price point channel, such as a discounted Internet travel site. This can be costly to any organization as the purchaser is using up considerable resources not dedicated to their actual point of purchase.

Nunes and Cespedes (2003) refer to this behavior as "value poaching." Given that channel choices are expanding, there is almost an infinite set of paths that a customer can take through a set of channels to complete a transaction. Therefore, organizations need to create enticements that draw customers through profitable paths. This is much different than shifting customers to low cost channels. Rather, this involves adding value to elements of the channel structure to encourage customer use for specific activities. It does not assume that some customers can be confined to specific channels.

Given that adding new channels rarely means taking old ones away, there needs to be careful planning and consideration to provide order for both customers and sales organizations in a state of ever-increasing complexity. This includes a supportive data infrastructure, skilled managers, guidelines for conflict resolution, and a customer-focused usage strategy. Organizations that are successful at this are those that are managing the use of channels to meet not only their individual expectations but also to fulfill the promise of a multichannel structure.

3

EXAMINING THE DEPLOYMENT OF SALES RESOURCES

*"We've changed the organization twice in the past 18 months. We've increased the
level of expertise in the direct sales force and we've added a whole new organization
focused on large accounts. We've evolved from a 'sell whatever you can' model
to a more strategic view of market and territory management."*

—Sales Director

As noted in Chapter 2, a direct sales force remains and will continue to remain a critical channel for selling organizations. This includes the use of field, or face-to-face, sales professionals as well as inside sales representatives. Strategies to best leverage the investment in a direct sales force varied by company. In fact, there was no single deployment strategy that dominated. What was consistent was that almost every organization we talked to was in the midst of restructuring their sales force and, furthermore, the constant changes in customer expectations, solution sets, and channel strategies render it very unlikely that any sales force deployment strategy could be considered permanent.

COMMON STRUCTURES

There are probably an infinite number of combinations to describe sales force deployment strategies. At the core, however, our study found four common strategies behind sales force allocation—product line, customer characteristics, geographic location, and sales activities. Each is described in detail below. Keep in mind, however, that deployments are rarely accomplished using only one method. It is most common to employ a matrix strategy; for example, deploy resources by potential in some tiers, others by geography, and others against highly technical product segments.

Product Line

Deploying a sales force by product line is one of the most traditional ways to go about allocating resources. It is beneficial in supplying high levels of product expertise to buying organizations. As organizations merge and extend solution sets into numerous lines, however, it becomes less common as a primary strategy. As a result of these mergers and investments, some of the sales organizations we studied found themselves in situations where they were deploying multiple sales representatives into the same customer account, each selling a different set of products. This created inefficiencies from both the selling and the buying perspectives. Customers were unable to form consistent experiences with brands, and business customers in particular were unable to satisfy the needs of centralized procurement departments. From the sales side, it created costly redundancies, fragmented the collection of customer information, and increased the cost of sales.

Another consideration is the sales strategy or approach being targeted by the selling organization. A sales force deployed against products, for example, would not be a good fit within an organization that is using bundling or other solutions-based approaches to the market. There are still many situations, however, where this strategy can work particularly well. For example, it is beneficial in cases where the product sales and

Moving Hewlett Packard from a Product-Oriented to a Customer-Oriented Sales Organization

As part of the new HP (post Compaq merger), a reorganization was undertaken to better deploy sales resources against customer segments. Under this new segmentation scheme, product divisions were assigned responsibility for selling into specific customer segments. For example, the Enterprise Systems Group (ESG), which focuses on system integration, outsourcing, and other elements of enterprisewide information technology (IT) infrastructure, was assigned as the primary interface to the corporate, enterprise, and commercial account bases. The Personal Systems Group (PSG) was assigned to manage vendor and distributor relationships and the Imaging and Printing Group (IPG) was accountable for the consumer side of the business. As a result of this restructuring, HP notes that "success is no longer owning a product line" and the sales force is able to "rally around the passion for the customer."

implementation may be highly technical or a great deal of product detail is involved in the buying process. Office Depot, for instance, supplements its main account representatives with salespeople who specialize in furniture sales. This product line requires interior design and other implementation factors not required with office supply purchases and therefore merits an additional contact point with the customer account. Another good example is Intier Automotive Inc., a Canadian supplier of interior and closure systems, that reports that it is moving to a more product-oriented deployment system to best represent the highly technical nature of its product line. This is also favored by its account base, which includes enormous organizations (the Big Three U.S. automakers, Toyota, BMW, Honda, etc.) divided into many specialized divisions. Given the technical detail needed in the purchasing process, there is less benefit to centralize purchasing with a single relationship manager across various divisions.

Customer Characteristics

Deploying sales resources against specific customer segments that exhibit common characteristics can be useful in creating specialization within the sales force and supporting organizational initiatives around customer centricity. Within our study, examples of this kind of deployment strategy used customer potential, industry, and buying preferences as a basis.

One common example of this can be found in the creation of sales teams to serve global or key accounts that are thought to have unique needs, have a greater desire for partnering, and are strategically important to the selling organization. This kind of global account strategy was once only used for a few top accounts within a selling organization. Today, however, many organizations in our study are beginning to deploy it within larger portions of their customer base. Typically, this can be beneficial for customers in that they are better able to receive coordinated service across a wide range of geographies instead of having to negotiate separate sales cycles in each region. From the seller side, this can be a valuable strategy for elevating influence and earning Trusted Business Advisor status within a high-potential account. Although this can be a resource-intensive strategy, as many of these key accounts will require access to product, finance, technical, and implementation specialists, it has the potential to yield high rewards.

This allocation by potential can extend beyond global accounts throughout the customer base. For example, global or key accounts may merit specialized sales teams; lesser potential accounts might be assigned individual account executives. Those with yet even less potential might most efficiently be handled through inside sales representatives or through other chan-

Global Account Teams at Marriott International

At part of a companywide "sales transformation" process, Marriott International created a Global Sales Organization (GSO) to serve the specific needs of very large business accounts. The largest of these accounts are considered to be "alliance accounts," which have specific needs associated with their high volume, distribution of product use (event planning, commercial travel, etc.), and business complexity. Furthermore, the buying process in these accounts occurs centrally and is based on a partnering model rather than standard procurement. In response, Marriott created global teams for these accounts in order to build and maintain strategic relationships at the highest levels of the organization and truly partner with a customer to best meet its business goals.

This kind of deployment requires sales resources that are capable of using advanced account management processes coupled with a consultative selling approach. Global account team members must be well-versed in business and financial topics, industry challenges, and opportunities, as well as in working in a global environment. For example, Marriott sales teams are able to provide value to alliance accounts by conducting research, surveying travelers, and analyzing travel spending, as well as by advising travel and event planners—well beyond traditional sales activities.

nels. This clearly has advantages for the selling organization in that lower potential customers can be served with lower cost of sale resources. The key is to ensure that this distinction is not perceived by customers as a lack of organizational commitment. Particularly as organizations change, care must be taken to ensure that customers do not feel slighted as their contact person changes. ("Hey, I used to get a face-to-face sales rep, now I only get a phone call!") Ensuring that the sales process and approach used within these different groups is aligned where appropriate can alleviate this problem.

Aligning Sales Resources to Customer Types
at TD Waterhouse

TD Waterhouse offers customers the best mix of products, price, and service based on their investment needs. For purely self-directed investors, the company offers a comprehensive online platform with premier research capabilities and a robust product lineup. For investors who require a bit more guidance, they have a dedicated branch network and TD Waterhouse Investment Centers. Finally, for those investors who prefer more of a "full service" experience and an advice-driven approach, TD Waterhouse has a network of independent advisors available. The company therefore deploys its sales resources and creates its channels to meet the unique needs of each of its customer segments.

Another example of segmentation based on customer characteristics is the pursuit of a vertical strategy. Although this is a resource-intensive strategy often executed within a separate business unit, vertical strategy offers many advantages by being able to link solutions to specific business issues that will resonate with members of an industry and can give organizations an advantage over generalist competitors. Vertically structured sales teams often have dedicated personnel who market, sell to, and support industry clients utilizing a customized marketing effort and solution set. Sales resources deployed against vertical structures are usually deeply embedded in the industry having worked in it prior.

Regardless of the specific method used, deploying sales resources by customer type usually involves advanced selling capabilities to reap the benefits. For example, salespeople acting as a single point of contact for the selling organization must be able to sell all product sets to the customer. Those managing global accounts must be able to influence the actions of virtual team members; those leading key account teams will need high levels of financial and business acumen. (More on "reskilling" the sales force is found in Chapter 6.)

Geographic Location

Segmenting sales teams by geography allows for extensive coverage, increased face time, and local responsiveness to customer issues. This strategy works best in situations where the sales force is tasked with selling a relatively homogenous product set to a broad customer base. Local presence can be particularly important as businesses cross international boundaries. Local resources will be much more in tune to cultural nuances and business etiquette. On the downside, as sales resources are widely dispersed across geographies, it becomes more difficult to identify and share best practices across sales teams.

As organizations have looked to ways to reduce the infrastructure expenditures required to serve a broad geographic deployment, they have frequently migrated to home office locations for their sales forces. This can be very effective but requires a good deal of planning and support. Key considerations include selection, management processes, and technological infrastructure. Some of the issues associated with home offices, include the following:

- Not all individuals will thrive when isolated from team members. At the same time, the lone-wolf salesperson may not be a good choice given a lack of direct oversight. Therefore, organizations prefer to hire and develop salespeople who are self-directed and often look for people who have previously worked in a remote environment.
- Managers will be more challenged to provide coaching to remote team members and will have to create opportunities, such as team meetings, client visits, and the like, where

Local Attention from Yellow Book USA

Yellow Book USA creates yellow pages directories that focus on specific geographies (e.g., Tampa, Florida, has a yellow pages directory; Long Island, New York, is covered by several directories). Yellow Book deploys a direct sales force to engage prospects to ensure adequate coverage of the directory's footprint. As Yellow Book feels its competitive advantage lies with its sales force, they want to get these people in front of as many customers as possible. Therefore, they deploy a large premise-based sales force to cover the directory markets and "swing every door."

This deployment strategy has been particularly beneficial in the small business segment where Yellow Book has been able to differentiate itself. While competitors largely employ telesales reps for account acquisition, Yellow Book is able to make a case to prospects that an in-person visit results in more personalized and value-added services. The message delivered is that "every account counts and we would never take one for granted, no matter how small."

they can observe, coach, and develop a salesperson. It will take extra managerial effort to be diligent around communication and performance management.
- Individuals in a home office environment will need hassle-free, fast, and secure access to e-mail, customer relationship management (CRM) systems, and other company systems in order to work efficiently.

Furthermore, organizations need to consider the cultural implications of a home-based sales force. There must be a more proactive onboarding process so that the salesperson has a real feel for what it means to sell for the organization. If they do not feel like an integrated part of the organization, they will be more likely to use inconsistent processes and deliver uncoordinated messages to customers, and may be unable to leverage organizational strengths (such as reputation and values) as differentiators in competitive selling situations.

Sales Activities

Some organizations are returning to a method of deploying sales resources based on their activity or role in the sales cycle. The most common method is called "hunters/farmers." This involves targeting a set of sales resources, "hunters," at prospecting and account acquisition activities and another set, "farmers," at account maintenance. This particular method has been tried off and on over the years, resurfacing in recent times as economic pressures have put a spotlight on the need for new business acquisition.

Organizations that are pursuing this route are working to make changes throughout the selling organization to support the shift. For example, from the human capital perspective, it requires a detailed skills assessment and the creation of job profiles, as well as revising performance management and other systems. Each type of resource must have clear direction on their role and responsibilities. Hunter resources will have to be sure to acquire quality business (rather than closing questionable deals that someone else will have to manage). On the other hand, farmer resources must be sure to continue to look for new opportunities in an account instead of functioning simply as order takers. As explained by one newly appointed hunter, "We are hunters for this company; we win new customers. We're not responsible for protecting a base. After two to three months, new customers are transferred to an inbound rep for retention. We were selected for this because we are aggressive, self-motivated team players." From an operational perspective, it involves a reengineering of processes (and often technological infrastructure) to support handoffs between sales resources and create a seamless customer experience, such that customers would not experience a decline in the level or quality of relationship as they are transitioned between sales resources.

WHICH TO CHOOSE?

A decision on how to deploy sales resources should be an output of more macro-level sales strategies. What do we sell? Who do we sell to? What value proposition are we offering to the marketplace? As such, there is no "right" way to deploy a sales force—it depends on what the organization is trying to accomplish. The key then becomes using a mixture of the strategies to create the right balance of effectiveness and efficiency—creating optimal relationships with customers while managing cost of sale appropriately. One common model observed in our study might be described in the following way:

- Formal, global account teams are created for each key account. These resources sell the entire breadth of products and services and are often assigned exclusively to one account.
- Geographically-managed field resources are given greater numbers of lesser potential accounts to manage—again selling the entire breadth of products and services.
- Regionally-located inside sales resources are targeted against large numbers (often 100–200) of even smaller sized clients.
- Distinct sales roles are created to sell specific, highly technical product suites to customers of all sizes.
- Other channels are used to handle the remaining customer segments.

As with all the strategies discussed in this text, this is an additive approach—more segments and structures are being added all of the time. This creates a very complex, matrixed organization and can create significant opportunity for inefficiencies and customer confusion. In a business sale, a large account could be engaged with a variety of salespeople in the same selling organization. For example, a local branch may be working with a local sales resource; the headquarters may be working with a key account team; yet other buying centers may be working with product-oriented sales resources. If not carefully coordinated, neither organization (buyer nor seller) will have a complete view of the relationship. This holds true for consumer selling models as well. Very often, a single consumer will be contacted by multiple resources from the same organization resulting in inefficiency and an inconsistent (and often frustrating) brand experience. As a result, the more complex the deployment strategy, the greater the need for clear account assignment and migration policies (i.e., who owns which account or customer segment and when does that account move from one segment to another—for example, from regional account to global account status).

Teaming: The More the Merrier?

Clearly, many of these constructs involve the use of teams. Permanent teams will be assembled to address ongoing circumstances or market conditions (e.g., creating a sales team to handle a key global account). Others are more temporary in nature, such as assembling a cross-functional team to create a sales proposal for a client. In either case, teams can be an effective way to achieve tasks that cannot be accomplished individually. On the other hand, poorly conceived or managed teams can be a great waste of resources. When assembling a team for selling purposes, ask yourself the following questions:

- *What is the business issue driving the creation of this team?* Too often teams are created without a unifying business purpose, resulting in a collective waste of time. Instead, each team should understand its charter and how it links to sales and corporate strategies.

- *What kind of work will this team be tasked with?* This will help determine what kind of team you need to assemble and who you need on it. For example, you may need to assemble a cross-functional team to function as a CRM advisory board. On the other hand, you may want to assemble a temporary team of senior salespeople to look into a mentoring program.
- *How will I assign roles and responsibilities?* Developing a specific team charter and assigning clear roles and responsibilities and performance metrics is critical to fostering consensus building and to preventing coasting, domination, or group think by team members.

Teaming at Fuji-Xerox

Tokyo-based Fuji-Xerox provides digital copying and publishing machines, networks, servers, and workstations, as well as other products and services associated with document services. Due to market demands for increasingly technical solutions, the company is more frequently utilizing a team-selling approach. Such teams are designed to combine individual strengths to create proposals and solutions for customers that leverage a full suite of products and solutions to create fully integrated network solutions. This has not only resulted in creating better proposals but also in reducing sales cycles because teams of salespeople collaborate to meet a client need. Further, by assigning teams to opportunities, the company can better represent its talent and implementation ability. As one sales manager noted, "We need to be able to make proposals that will bring changes in a customer's operations, rather than proposals explaining our product's features and benefits. So a team-selling approach has become more and more important for us because it can show our strengths in process improvement and reform."

- *How will customers be impacted?* If different members of a team will be interacting with a customer at different points in the sales cycle (e.g., pairs of hunters and farmers), then it pays to ensure that there are processes in place to guarantee a smooth handoff.
- *Does my organization support teaming?* Individuals should be prepared to work successfully in teams. Make sure training provides the base for acquiring the proper skills in the areas of collaboration, communication, negotiation, and influencing.
- *How will compensation be handled?* When we spoke with organizations that had failed with specific team constructs, we found compensation was often to blame, specifically in situations where sales teams shared a quota and shared compensation. Under those plans, there was very little individual accountability and high inconsistency in contribution.

Looking beyond the Sales Organization

Another factor to consider when deploying the sales force is those relationships that must be formed with internal stakeholders in functional areas outside of the sales organization. Such stakeholders include, but are not limited to, customer service, finance, legal, marketing, fulfillment, and product development. Over time, these departments have migrated from operating as individual silos to becoming more integrated—using the customer experience as a focal point.

This creates both benefit and additional responsibility for the sales force. Unlike no other time in the past, sales professionals find themselves in a position of being able to truly leverage the efforts undertaken by other functions in the organization. This is most clear in the integration of sales and marketing. When operating in tandem with the marketing department, sales forces can leverage market research, competitive analysis, and customer segmentation to sell more effectively and efficiently. At the same time, the sales force bears a greater accountability for delivering customer information back to these departments to ensure that the customer's point of view is adequately reflected in all aspects of front- and back-office activity (supports servicing activity, market research, etc.). As one marketing executive noted, "Sales gives us input into what they need to sell our products. We have regular meetings together—to educate each other about what we are working on and what they say their customers want. This way we can build off each other instead of working at odds."

Structurally then, it becomes important to formally create these links and support the needed processes so that the sales organization maintains insight into, influences, and leverages the functional initiatives and processes in these areas. This is critical because, as noted previously, decisions about sales force structure cannot be made in a vacuum. For example, if the marketing organization is structured by product type, it then becomes difficult to have a vertical-based sales strategy that sells solutions based on industry business issues.

Organizations we worked with were using a variety of techniques to better leverage other parts of their organization. Some were temporarily rotating sales and marketing management for cross training. Others were including marketing managers on sales calls. Yet others were building cross-functional teams tasked with collecting and analyzing customer feedback. Even if a formal mechanism was not in place, individual salespeople were reaching out to other parts of the organization to mine their expertise. One example, which illustrates this well, was a Diebold salesperson who said that he always recommended visiting the technicians and talking to them about their experiences in working with automated teller machines (ATMs) at client sites. This helped him identify potential issues as well as new opportunities in accounts.

BEST PRACTICES AND LESSONS LEARNED

The clearest conclusion from our observations on sales structure is that change in this area is constant; it's likely your sales force will be segmented and redeployed on an ongoing basis. Therefore, the key is to create flexibility to support shifts in deployment. At the same time, recognize that churning salespeople can alienate the customer base and can dismantle a sales culture. As such, change management considerations should be integrated into the restructuring activity and structures should be designed in support of organizational agility.

Tips for guiding restructuring activity include:

- Acknowledge the difficulty of change and prepare your salespeople and your customers to navigate it (early and ongoing communication is critical).
- Explain the benefits to customers (perhaps they will be getting a more local or more specialized resource).
- Explain the benefits to salespeople (better targeting means more face time and more revenues, less travel time, more support).
- Be able to clearly explain the impact on performance evaluation (as the saying goes, people do what is "inspected" not what is "expected").
- Build a plan to ensure that the next salesperson has a warm transition (this may call for an in-person introduction by the current salesperson) and just as importantly has access to all of the relevant data.
- Build consistency into operations across the sales structure so that if a person changes sales teams, processes and systems do not have to be relearned. This will reduce ramp-up time.
- Put specific territory guidelines in place to minimize conflict among the various parts of the structure.

- Create formal mechanisms for uncovering best practices and replicating them across different parts of the sales force. Some structures will lend themselves to this kind of communication and some will not. The key is to make it happen anyway.
- Give salespeople a greater sense of the organization. If their only relationship to an organization is with a particular selling team, then they will become disenfranchised as they are moved to different parts of the sales organization.

In addition to ensuring a smooth transition, special care should be taken to make sure that no matter what their position in the new structure, all sales professionals feel part of the bigger team. Too often, organizations continue to structure themselves in ways that discourage this, building silos only to tear them down again in a self-defeating cycle.

LEVERAGING TECHNOLOGIES FOR SALES SUCCESS

"You need a very, very clear vision of the desired output of the sales technology system and have to start there. What are you going to get out of it? What do the salespeople get? How will it help customers? Once you have defined the output, it becomes much easier to train the sales force on the input."

—Sales Manager

At least since the mid-1980s organizations have been trying to figure out how to best leverage technologies to improve the sales process, create better relationships with customers, and ultimately grow revenue. With incredible advances in computer and software technologies taking place almost overnight, companies didn't have long to figure out how to best leverage the tools available to them. Nearly two decades later many organizations still have not figured it out, yet this comes as little surprise when one considers the rapid growth in the size and complexity of data requirements as well as the business process and human-related challenges of implementing enterprisewide technologies. Today, however, given ever growing market challenges, organizations have no choice but to optimize sales technologies. As the organizations in our study demonstrate, technology strategies to manage customer relationships and automate sales activities are critical requirements to compete.

Since the term was first used sometime in the mid-1990s, customer relationship management, or CRM, has been defined as relating to almost every element of business that even remotely touches a customer. The term has been mentioned in thousands of articles and books, and has been heralded and criticized by technology experts, salespeople, and executives alike. As a subset of CRM, the concept of sales force automation (SFA) has been discussed just as often and sometimes (incorrectly) used interchangeably with the term CRM. As part of the broader sales technology movement of the past two decades, applications relating to sales activities and customer data have evolved over the years from simple contact management to complex software integrating product, customer, and supplier data.

By the mid-1990s, it became clear that few organizations could compete without adopting some level of software- and hardware-enabled sales automation or CRM system. Indeed, a technology system that maximizes the relationship with the customer is critical for remaining competitive and providing the level of sales and service that customers have come to expect. This comes with new requirements in terms of skills, daily sales activities, organizational communication and support, and the like. As one organization's representative remarked, "In the past, you only needed to know how to use a copy machine. Today you need to manage e-mail, electronic calendars, to-do lists, databases, and more."

This chapter focuses on the strategies companies have adopted around the development and implementation of CRM and SFA systems, and it reviews the challenges and successes experienced by the organizations we studied. Although the organizations in this study were at different stages of CRM implementation at the time of the interviews, many of them share common challenges, strategies, and keys to success regardless of their size, industry, or technological sophistication.

While most organizations we studied were in the later stages of CRM implementation, no company, not even the most high-tech ones, considered their system implementation to be complete. This suggests that there may be no end state for CRM, but rather with more market challenges and rapid advances in technology, the best CRM strategy will be one that is flexible and constantly adapting to new environments. The organizations studied that were in earlier stages of CRM implementation shared with us the valuable lessons they were learning along the way. In addition, several organizations recently experiencing mergers or acquisitions were confronted with yet another set of technology challenges, including data compatibility issues and the integration of legacy systems. Across all cases, our interview findings suggest that implementing sales technology is difficult and time-consuming, but not impossible if organizations account for the critical business and human requirements for success. This chapter highlights the strategies leading sales organizations have pursued in an effort to finally get it right.

TECHNOLOGY AND THE SUCCESSFUL SALES ORGANIZATION

If you ask ten people to define CRM, or for that matter, SFA, you will likely get ten different definitions. Although no two definitions are alike, there emerges some common language demonstrating that the concept, from both a technology and a process standpoint, is becoming more focused.

Pulling together common themes across dozens of definitions, broadly speaking, CRM can be defined as any information technology (IT) that helps an organization overall and the sales division in particular execute processes for developing and sustaining long-term, profitable customer relationships. More specifically, CRM is a corporate strategy and a corresponding system of tools and procedures a firm uses to identify, locate, acquire, and retain customers, as well as manage interactions with customers at several touch points.

SFA, as a subset of CRM, refers to a system of hardware and software applications that automate a wide range of sales activities, but differs from CRM in that it may not involve other non-sales activities and databases within the organization. As the technology and process, and hence a definition of the concepts of CRM and SFA, have developed, there is a consensus that CRM should add value to the customer, increase the value of the customer to the seller, and create efficiencies and improve effectiveness of serving customers for the salesperson and the organization as a whole.

When most people think of CRM, they are generally referring to the various software and hardware incorporated in an enterprisewide system. However, a CRM system also involves the processes by which organizations interact with and collect data on their customers and prospects. These include sales processes, ordering, customer service, and marketing processes among others. Many argue that a CRM system is indeed more than just software and hardware, but rather it encompasses extensive changes within a company in terms of skills, processes, and structures. CRM tools merely enable and enhance these attributes.

This chapter explores what we found to be the prerequisites of a successful CRM strategy—having effective and efficient business and sales processes in place, understanding beforehand the required business outcomes of the system, ensuring that the right skills are in the right place, and leveraging the right hardware and software tools to execute these processes.

Sales Technology: Hardware, Software, and Process

CRM went through several stages from the mid-1980s through the 1990s, from systems designed to automate a few sales activities, to sophisticated databases and data collection processes encompassing all types of customer and product data. The evolution to full-blown CRM systems by the late 1990s reflected the realization that there are many touch points with the customer and that more fully understanding customer behavior allowed better forecasting and the ability to establish strategies that mutually serve the needs and expectations of the buyer and seller. Organizations assumed even more of an external or customer-centric perspective focusing on such things as what the customer buys and when, why, and for how much; what creates value for customers; and what drives their buying decisions. CRM systems also ensured that organizations had stable relationships with customers across sales channels and that customers had similar experiences across sales channels.

The idea was to enhance the quality of every customer interaction by ensuring that everyone in the organization who comes in contact with customers can access accurate information at the right time. CRM became the most important data management tool available to organizations as they faced an incredible growth in the complexity and sheer volume of customer data.

Sales technologies that compose CRM and SFA systems include both hardware and software that allows salespeople to input, record, track, and recall customer- and product-related information. Hardware typically includes laptops, cell phones, personal digital assistants (PDAs), and presentation equipment. Software includes PC-based applications automating a host of sales and business activities, complex database software, and wireless business intelligence that includes access to data via wireless communications. Figure 4.1 shows the percentage of salespeople reporting that their organization offers various sales technology–related applications.

Web-based applications, or eCRM technology, include electronic commerce ordering, product configuration, pricing, and tracking and billing. In addition, eCRM also promotes marketing and sales efforts, such as electronic customized newsletters, e-mail communications, co-browsing, and product or service

FIGURE 4.1 Technologies Offered by Companies to Support the Sales Organization

Which of the following technologies does your company offer to support the sales organization?

Technology	%	Technology	%
E-mail	93%	Price quote	30%
Web site	76	Forecasting	28
Contact management	54	Online order entry	24
Electronic forms	48	Automated call reporting	21
Online product information	44	Automated proposal	
Scheduling/time management	42	generations	21

offerings provided electronically that are based on predictive behavioral models. As more organizations establish a presence on the Web, competition requires dependable and robust interactive e-commerce capabilities. Through an eCRM system, this "channel" of data flowing to and from customers is integrated with other databases and customer touch points within the organization, such as customer service, telesales/marketing, and direct sales.

MARKET CHALLENGES AND THE SALES TECHNOLOGY SOLUTION

Increasingly demanding and more knowledgeable customers, global competition, and price pressures are just a few of the significant market challenges organizations in our study face today. These business challenges, and those mentioned in Chapter 3, will continue to drive organizations to become more efficient and effective in creating lasting and valuable relationships with customers. As products become more commoditized and prices become more transparent, organizations must differentiate themselves in the marketplace and sell on the additional value they can bring to their customer.

Computer technology and the Internet have profoundly changed the way customers buy because their access to a wide range of detailed product, pricing, and competitive information gives them a distinct advantage vis-à-vis suppliers. Access to this information decreases switching costs, provides more options to customers, and allows customers to play competitors off each other to gain the best deal. Organizations in our study see this development as both a challenge and an opportunity. Intier Automotive Inc., a Canadian supplier of interiors and closure systems to the major North American original equipment manufacturers (OEMs), said that smarter customers have put the pressure on both themselves and carmakers as they noted, "The way the Internet has affected us is now we have smarter consumers—those who purchase vehicles. With the Internet they can access safety ratings and learn about new features like SUV folding or removable seats. They don't have to wait for the next consumer product reviews. They know what they want and who has what to offer." According to Intier Automotive, as a result, OEMs are placing more pressure on them to be a full-service supplier and to know what end users want and need.

Another important reason organizations must have a good sales technology strategy is the complex nature of data and service requirements stemming from the growth in outsourcing and the multiple relationships that customers and suppliers are creating across each other's organization. Particularly for strategic key accounts, though even for transactional customers, there are many touch points within the supplier organization. For example, multiple sales channels (phone, Web, in person), product ordering, shipping/delivery, and after-sales service all represent activities within an organization that exchange data with customers.

A companywide CRM system is critical for managing data flowing to and from the customer at multiple points within the company. It reduces coordination errors between external sales

Low-Tech Business Benefits from High-Tech CRM: Yellow Book USA

When it comes to sales activities, high technology has not played much of a role in selling yellow pages advertising to small businesses. Indeed, Yellow Book USA, the largest non-Bell publisher of yellow pages, has done well as a relatively low-tech, paper-based organization. Small business customers are not technologically sophisticated—"they are pen-and-pencil type of businesses," and computers and other technologies do not sit well in face-to-face sales calls with small "mom and pop" businesses.

This view is changing, however, as Yellow Book explores the opportunities of applying technology to manage the customer relationship process and automate daily activities for improving the effectiveness and efficiency of servicing customers. The company is rolling out a CRM system that will be able to "control and pinpoint specifics of the marketplace and automate many sales activities." According to one respondent, "This system gives the management team the opportunity to develop the market and find areas that have been missed." Although Yellow Book "will never be at the cutting edge of technology, and it may be some time before the field is completely automated, the system will provide salespeople with more capabilities for managing their territory, accounts, and selling activities."

The system will be used for customer account history, payment status, and allowing representatives to pull customer's artwork off a computer to take with them on the sales call. The system will be used by sales, the inbound call center, and service and collections. According to one respondent, "[W]e know what advertising companies buy and when they buy it, and we have been doing a lot of systems integration over the past few years that have enabled consistent sales reporting and tracking. But the new system will do more to enable sales reps to cross-sell across territories and allow management to identify trends as they arise."

New technology being developed also will allow the sales representative to "key in contracts at the end of the day and the system would electronically identify errors or exceptions rather than having checkers manually proof documents." As one executive noted, "Eventually, contracts, artwork, everything will be online, but it may be a few years before we have that." Ultimately, according to one manager, "Moving toward a single platform for all sales activities will achieve economies of scale and increase customer face time."

and office-based personnel, between different sales teams, and between other functional areas with responsibility for customer interaction. For instance, when a customer accesses product information over the Internet and purchases by phone, that product and price data must be consistent. Customers have come to expect "seamless" sales and service from suppliers irrespective of the channel or point of contact.

Technology for Salespeople, Customers, and the Organization

The successful CRM system creates a powerful link between suppliers and customers, allowing better decisions for salespeople, customers, and the supplier because it enables enhanced processes that rely on data. For the salesperson, these decisions include targeting customers, and planning and optimizing customer interaction management. For the customer, decisions are enhanced around optimal product selection, solution configuration, and optimal post-sales service. For the organization, CRM both increases knowledge of customers and sales activities in the field and improves decision making regarding optimal pricing, product configuration, service options, and sales strategies.

The salesperson benefits from increased efficiency—executing sales activities faster and at a lower cost—and improved effectiveness—doing things better. CRM systems allow salespeople to more easily qualify customers with greater accuracy, and to improve leads and customer selection/targeting information through development of large customer databases. Many of the organizations we studied expected that their CRM system would eventually allow the salesperson to more quickly produce complex proposals that required input from various parts of the organization, configure products more accurately and rapidly, and address special pricing and delivery needs. Automated ordering, invoicing, and tracking systems also can reduce cycle time and overall costs of sales. (See Figure 4.2.)

While increasing the efficiency and effectiveness of sales activities should make life easier for salespeople, many organizations have not yet realized this potential. According to a Selling Power/AchieveGlobal (Selling Power, 2002) study, only 36 percent of salespeople were very or somewhat satisfied that technology improved their overall job performance, and only 30 percent were very or somewhat satisfied that technology improved the sales process.

For customers, CRM capabilities can provide more information for making buying decisions through better access to

---

FIGURE 4.2 Benefits of Sales Technologies

Somewhat Agree or Strongly Agree That Sales Technologies . . .

Improve communication within the sales organization.	73%	Improve product appeal.	56%
Improve communication with the customer.	70	Improve ability to attract and meet more potential customers.	56
Improve my relationship with the customer.	62	Increase sales with new customers.	55
Improve my ability to develop my sales strategy.	61	Reduce order processing time.	50
Increase sales with existing customers.	59	Reduce proposal/quote preparation time.	49
Reduce call preparation and documentation time.	58	Reduce nonproductive calls/leads.	43
		Improve account receivable cycle time.	41

accurate and current data on product selection, price, and availability. It also can make ordering, payment, and post-sales service more effective and efficient. Ideally, for the customer, there is a seamless interface irrespective of the sales channel and easier product selection, configuration, and compatibility that may involve electronic catalogs, mockups, virtual designs, and customer input capabilities. Faster and easier access regarding bids, ordering, tracking, delivery, inventory levels, and electronic invoicing are hallmarks of a successful CRM system.

CRM is capable of allowing customers to enjoy the same level of service regardless of the sales channel. Successful organizations have integrated their customer servicing and problem resolution processes into their overall CRM system. At Marriott, CRM "provides seamless customer interactions across sales channels without having to ask the customer the same questions and reenter data." TD Waterhouse credits its CRM system with "moving the company's brokers from mere order takers to being more proactive in their customer service and selling efforts."

Finally, successful CRM implementation also benefits the organization overall, and sales management in particular. Because at the core of CRM is customer data, sales managers can more effectively monitor sales activities and their salesperson's performance, and assess stages of the sales cycles with individual customers, allowing managers to provide better coaching and forecasting. Sales managers at TD Waterhouse are better able to keep track of customer call notes and guide brokers to pay attention to the right customers. This has resulted in reduced down times and helped them to move leads along more quickly. According to the organizations in our study, management's access to this information also eliminates the "island of information problem" and improves institutional knowledge by collecting databases that salespeople populate.

While there have been claims that these capabilities have led to "micromanagement" by sales managers, several organizations in our study claim just the opposite. Stora Enso, an international manufacturer of forest products, said that its CRM allows managers to view information from a "more strategic, big-picture perspective, thus eliminating the need for managers to question salespeople or observe closely day-to-day sales activities, which takes time for both salespeople and managers and disrupts the work flow." For many of the organizations we spoke with, CRM was designed as an effective coaching tool for management rather than merely an oversight mechanism.

TECHNOLOGY STRATEGIES FOR SUCCESSFUL SALES

According to most accounts, CRM implementations more often fail than succeed. In fact, it is estimated that anywhere between 65 percent to 75 percent of all implementations fail to meet initial expectations. We are reminded of this almost daily by the experts, as noted by the following:

- Gschwandter (2001) showed that two-thirds of CRM installations failed to meet all goals, almost half were late, and more than a third over budget.
- According to Costello (2000), out of 50 large CRM users, 90 percent admitted to not being able to measure a tangible return from CRM implementation.
- Another study (Zoltners, 2001) reported that 70 percent of firms had little or no improvement as a result of CRM implementation.

Not only do CRM and SFA failures—or those implementations merely not meeting expectations—cost the company money, the opportunity costs of forgoing the benefits of a fully functional system can be staggering. A consulting study reported by Thompson (2003) concluded that a typical company with $1 billion in revenue could increase profits up to $130 million by improving their CRM system, and that CRM explained as much as two-thirds of the difference in return on sales between average and high performing organizations.

Despite the benefits, except for the largest organizations, most organizations do not have a fully functional CRM system in place, and many are not even planning one. A recent online poll by CRMCommunity.com (2003) showed that 47 percent of organizations had no plan to implement CRM in the coming year, 42 percent planned to in the near future, and only 9 percent had already fully implemented a CRM system. Most of the organizations in our study had implemented or were in the process of implementing a CRM system.

Participating organizations shared with us both the challenges and the keys to success that they experienced throughout their sales technology implementation. The next section discusses some of the challenges we heard about in our interviews and, more importantly, the strategies for successfully preparing the organization for change, designing the right system, and executing the rollout. While this chapter considers CRM and its subset SFA systems as important sales strategies, the following sections discuss the challenges and critical success factors with implementing broader CRM systems. However, the lessons apply to more sales department–specific SFA applications because they are often embedded in more organization-wide CRM systems.

Preparing the Organization for Success

Organizational factors, such as current sales skills, sales force segmentation, customer relationship processes, past experiences with sales force technologies, and other cultural variables, all have a bearing on the degree to which organizations can leverage their CRM systems.

Many of the organizations participating in the study had implemented or attempted to implement sales force technologies in the past, and many efforts were met with mixed results. The historical experience with sales force technologies has a significant impact on subsequent implementations. We found that bad experiences make it extremely difficult to create support and confidence among salespeople for a new system. A reputation of failed experiments fosters the "here we go again" attitude. One salesperson remarked, "I approach this stuff with a 'this too shall pass' attitude. . . . I'll wait it out and they'll roll something else out a year from now." To overcome this, leaders must be able to demonstrate causes for past failures, show how and why things will be different the next time around, and allow required business outcomes to drive system development rather than the other way around.

The most effective way to overcome negative experiences is creating a sales culture that will embrace change, understand clearly the advantages and limitations of technology, and involve the trust of leaders. This cultural preparedness also involves leaders building a case for implementing a new system,

O vercoming the Past at Diebold

Diebold, the manufacturer of bank security systems, automated teller machines (ATMs), and election systems, is currently undergoing its largest ever software automation and integration initiative. Based on an *Oracle I Ii* CRM platform, the company will integrate processes and information to allow "salespeople to achieve balance, become more productive, and make their lives easier, as well as to better serve customers." The goal is to let salespeople organize customer information and ultimately have more time in front of the customer.

In the past, Diebold had mixed results implementing sales technologies, and as a result, some in the sales organization were initially skeptical of the most recent initiative. The general feeling was that often technology "hurts us because it requires effort and time and we don't always have an opportunity to understand the value of how it helps our job." In addition, past efforts ignored problems with sales processes. One respondent said, "Every time we roll something out it ends up being more of a burden than a help, probably because we automated the current process as opposed to fixing the process and then automating it. For example, in the past, we took order-taking responsibilities off of less expensive resources and put them on the expensive sales resource."

Given the perceived lack of benefits to sales professionals, the lack of sales force input into SFA decisions, the mixed results of previous implementations, and the large concentration of tenured employees, some suspicion and initial push back was not surprising. As one respondent noted, "The record to date has been mediocre at best for getting systems out on time and with the desired functionality. We've been tinkering with the SFA system for six years." Agrees another, "Salespeople do not use existing systems as often as they should."

Diebold is very cognizant of these past missteps and is planning the current CRM implementation much more meticulously. As a result, the Oracle rollout is being viewed as a more thought-out process, and perceived as working more smoothly than past implementations.

These efforts are paying off. The sales organization is fully supporting the initiative and upper-level management is ensuring ongoing communication of the message that this will be a positive step for the company. Respondents mentioned that, in general, "this rollout has more upfront sales feedback preventing larger problems later."

Maintaining realistic expectations, Diebold believes that it may "go back a little before it goes forward" with the Oracle implementation because it touches every part of the company and it will take time to ramp up. However, the expectation is that they will be able to utilize pilot tests to identify all of the "gotchas and glitches" in a safe environment, instead of out in the field, thus allowing a more effective launch. As one respondent said, "The challenge is to convince salespeople that these are productivity enhancers to their lives and livelihood." From all accounts, the salespeople seem convinced and are on track for a successful implementation.

communicating a need for new processes and procedures, and clearly demonstrating the gains in the effectiveness and efficiency of sales activities and advantages for the customer. The most effective way to build and sell a case is to avoid "top-down" commands of how things will be and instead create trust by gaining input from users and stakeholders, and offering ownership in the decision-making process.

A handful of salespeople we interviewed felt that the sales technology was merely a tool for management to spy on what salespeople were doing. This "big brother" mentality is not a function of CRM technology but rather stems from a cultural predisposition for mistrust. Others looked at CRM as making salespeople redundant. One salesperson remarked, "I know why the organization does this stuff. They want to make sure that when the account rep leaves, all of their information is left behind. It's to make us expendable." For the organization to be ready to change, however, there must be a culture of trust between management and salespeople.

Before organizations embark on a CRM project, it is imperative that they have well-defined and clearly understood business and sales processes in place. Automating poorly performing activities and processes rarely improves the quality of the outcome. Leaders should have a good idea of how salespeople sell, how their customers buy, and how they need to service clients to create long-term loyalty. Many organizations participating in our study segment their sales force based on customer buying behavior, ranging from high-touch, key customers to those who are strictly transactional. The important human dimension here is that the skills required of salespeople in each segment must be defined and in place. Those salespeople dedicated to strategic selling to enterprise accounts must possess advanced sales skills including negotiation, resource management, internal networking, financial acumen, and the like, that salespeople selling to transactional customers do not need. Even beyond just the sales force, the skill requirements and processes at all customer touch points must be developed and clearly articulated before designing a CRM system.

While preparing the organization, companies must first be able to answer the following questions:

- What are the outcomes needed to move forward with a customer?
- What skills do people need, in all areas of the organization, that touch the customer?
- What information is needed from the customer?
- What information needs to get to the customer?
- What tools are needed to perform these tasks?

CRM systems then should be designed to improve the efficiency and effectiveness of the touch points and processes. Just overlaying a CRM technology where skills are not aligned and the right processes are not implemented will merely result in automation of bad processes.

Designing a Successful System

Organizations designing sales force technologies generally rely on a combination of outsourcing and homegrown or customized solutions. The Selling Power/AchieveGlobal study found that 30 percent of the organizations responding to the survey outsourced their entire sales technology system, 25 percent developed it completely in-house, and 46 percent both outsourced and built part of the system themselves. The organizations interviewed for this study generally mirrored these findings, with most purchasing software from a major supplier and customizing parts to meet their needs.

One of the critical success factors at the design phase is to ensure that the applications and functionality of the proposed system align with real everyday sales activities. Too often software applications are adopted merely because they are available, yet they have no relevancy for day-to-day sales activities. Sales technologies must improve job performance, but applications that are not directly aligned with improving the effectiveness or efficiency of sales activities end up as useless icons cluttering the desktop. One company we interviewed was working to pare down the number of software applications available to salespeople, eliminating those that were not needed. According to one of its managers, "Moving from more than two dozen icons on our sales force laptops to just the ten that we use saves us time and money, and just makes sense." According to the study by Selling Power/AchieveGlobal, 20 percent of salespeople said that they do not use their CRM system because the technology is not applicable to their sales activities.

Another question to consider is whether a full-blown CRM system is even required, given the organization's sales model, the nature of the business, or the size of the market. Infineum, a leading multinational manufacturer of fuel and lubricant additives, is experiencing consolidation among customers and has determined that a highly automated system is not required. With only a handful of customers and "six business processes," including such things as pricing, tender management, proposal generation, and the like, Infineum does not need a complex software system. This case reinforces the importance of designing a system that fits the needs of the sales organization rather than designing the organization to fit the needs of a system.

As the organization aligns the requirements and capabilities of CRM projects with business processes, it is critical that they remain realistic about what the system should and will do. Many companies make the mistake of over designing their system and developing well-intended yet unrealistic applications—those that are too time-consuming to use or create additional work. A salesperson from a participating company in the study noted, "I found it troublesome to input my data just to get the manager's feedback to my report. When the content is urgent, I communicate directly with my manager, but for less important cases, it is difficult for a manager to find time to give feedback. If a manager has 8 salespeople under him and each of them makes 10 entries a day, the manager must give feedback to 80 histories every day. If they don't give any feedback, team members will not be motivated and won't care to input the calls, which may cause a vicious circle."

Overengineered processes—those trying to do more than what is required by the business—are generally not user-friendly for salespeople and others in the organization who will be responsible for interacting with customers or customer data. For there to be full adoption and compliance, the design phase must ensure an easy to use, intuitive system. The Selling Power/AchieveGlobal study found that only 30 percent were satisfied or very satisfied that their company's sales technologies were convenient and easy to use, and 55 percent said that technologies that are too time-consuming or inconvenient to use is the number one barrier to adoption of technology within their organization.

A large office products retailer developed a comprehensive sales force application that contains key customer and prospect data, such as contact information, contact notes, order history, including products purchased and charges incurred, contract terms, delivery point information, invoicing, and purchase forecasting. However, the system was not being used by all of the salespeople because, as one respondent said, "It was heavy on the 'admin' side." Another application designed by the company allowing salespeople to track customer orders and related bonus/commission earnings was criticized by some as being cumbersome and inconvenient to use. Overdesigning the system and creating burdensome processes will lead to what one company in our study characterized as "too many inputs for the outputs you get."

Several of the organizations interviewed recently experienced a merger or acquisition. Attempting to integrate disparate sales technologies and back-office databases and systems adds an additional level of complexity to the design phase. Yellow Book USA, Stora Enso, Infineum, and Hewlett Packard all acquired or merged with other organizations in the recent past, though each company maintained realistic expectations of the time and effort required to fully integrate all legacy systems on one CRM platform.

As system requirements are being defined in the design phase, organizations must keep in mind that the most valuable design information will come from stakeholders and users. The sales organization should be the driver of the design phase and not merely along for the ride. This should begin with early solicitation of input from users and stakeholders, especially sales managers. Systems that are designed from the top down and forced on the salespeople without addressing their pain points or fitting easily into their daily work flow will result in poor adoption rates.

Successful organizations begin the design phase with answers to the following questions in mind:

- What features of the system will increase adoption?
- When do sales representatives prefer to do various sales activities, such as their call reporting?
- What information do salespeople really value in the field?

Intier Automotive's Strategies for Improving Usage of CRM

Intier Automotive Inc., the Canadian supplier of interior and closure systems for vehicles, has made considerable investments in sales technology. Most notable is the company's CRM software application known as Auto-

CRM. AutoCRM is a comprehensive application that contains key customer and prospect data, such as contact information, meeting notes, order history, pricing data, and data for forecasting purposes.

"Our new AutoCRM will help with sharing pricing information, contact information, and the like; will help us with the forecasting of new programs and auto models; and will allow us to choose and identify those programs that are important to us, such as the Dodge Ram pickup truck, for example." Another application involves virtual information sharing. As one respondent describes the application, "We had several teams from DaimlerChrysler, Ford, BMW, and others across Europe and North America on a conference call. In the past, they would have to run reports in advance of the meeting. Now they can log in to AutoCRM with their laptops or desktops and with a simple projector show the reports on a screen for all to see simultaneously."

Although respondents noted that AutoCRM will be very beneficial to the organization once it is fully implemented, there was initial resistance on the part of some salespeople to fully utilize the system. The company acknowledged this and immediately took steps to increase usage. The company is studying an innovative approach to reducing an account manager's administrative AutoCRM responsibilities. To ease the laborious task of entering meeting notes, for example, the company is beta testing a program that provides account managers with a pocket PC to orally record customer meeting notes. In addition, the company has identified the top ten customer issues and has asked its account managers to keep all customer notes within the range of those issues. The recorded information is later typed by other parties, sent back to the account manager via e-mail for confirmation, and then finally entered into AutoCRM.

While manufacturing and cost pressures are front and center issues for Intier, AutoCRM is an important tool for improving the customer relationship process. In the end, for it to be a success, the system must be seen as "valuable to salespeople's everyday activities and valuable to the customer as well." With encouragement from senior leaders, Intier is on its way to achieving this objective.

Designers must meet with salespeople to identify common frustrations and explore how best to fix them, and to determine what barriers are coming between the salesperson and the customer. For example, if the salesperson has not been able to access the most up-to-date marketing, product, and pricing information in the field, it is likely that he or she might have difficulty answering customers' questions.

Implementing a Successful System

Long after the concept and design have been developed, after vendors are selected and requirements identified, organizations are faced with creating a rollout plan, piloting a rollout, and, finally, implementing the CRM system throughout the organization. The implementation phase is generally the most painstaking and time-consuming. Observers agree that the process takes anywhere from a year to 18 months, and many of the organizations we studied expected their CRM to be fully online from 1 to 2 years after the design phase was completed. In a recent study of small and medium-sized businesses, Schaaf (2004) found that 30 percent of the organizations had completed their CRM deployment, 12 percent were in the process of rolling it out, 25 percent planned their implementation for the coming year, and more than a quarter (28 percent) had no plans to implement a CRM system.

This phase is difficult because training and support plans are being developed and executed, salespeople are trying to figure out what it all means to them, and various parts of the organization unaccustomed to working together must coordinate efforts in new ways. According to one company we interviewed, "When the rubber hits the road, there's some confusion. Everyone knows it's coming, but once it does it takes a while for everyone to figure out what to do and for things to start operating normally." How do organizations overcome these challenges in the implementation phase?

First and foremost, it is critical that organizations set realistic time lines and articulate clear goals and expectations for what they are trying to achieve throughout the rollout phase. Unrealistic time lines create frustration and ultimately damage the credibility of the project and confidence on the part of salespeople. Goal expectations should include specifics on who will be required to do what and when once the system is up and running. Salespeople will need to have a clear understanding of when they will be trained, when they will be required to use the system, and the implications of not using the system, and an understanding of how technologies will impact their roles and responsibilities. Salespeople must understand what it means for their workload, compensation, and responsibilities.

During the pilot and any phased rollout stages, salespeople are exposed live to the system for the first time. The level of comfort and competency that salespeople have with using the system is a critical factor for ensuring compliance. Many organizations have problems with getting their salespeople comfortable and competent during the rollout phase. According to the study by Schaaf, of the more than 500 IT professionals surveyed, more than half (59 percent) said that their company is somewhat comfortable or very comfortable using their CRM system, and only 55 percent said their company is somewhat competent or very competent in using the system. With only around half of all salespeople feeling comfortable with and skilled in using their CRM system, it is little wonder why adoption rates are so low.

One of the important lessons learned from organizations participating in our study is that management and senior leaders in the organization must be brand champions of the implementation, and they must encourage the organization to embrace the new system. According to Schaaf, 70 percent of all respondents agreed or strongly agreed that their senior leadership demonstrated commitment to their organization's CRM implementation. Leaders must create excitement and build momentum with continuous updates of the rollout. Management at Diebold, the manufacturer of ATM machines and bank security equipment, embodied the meaning of brand champions. They were able to describe the vision of the implementation and passionately communicate its benefits to the organization and their customers.

With leadership's commitment to a successful implementation comes systematic, clear, and ongoing communications throughout the organization. Company CRM newsletters, regular meetings, e-mails, and periodic updates of the rollout's progress are means by which successful organizations keep the rollout in the limelight, keep everyone informed, and maintain the momentum of excitement.

Early in the implementation phase, successful organizations design a training program plan that includes a curriculum, a selection of trainers and trainees, and a training schedule. While the software vendor often provides education, for most organizations there is a component that must be customized and, over time, the company assumes full responsibility for ongoing training. Training should include both technical and process competencies as well as how salespeople can get the most out of the system for themselves and their customers. Although most organizations provide training—more than two-thirds of organizations surveyed by Schaaf provided ongoing training to their employees—some organizations only provide basic training.

In addition to education, organizations that successfully implement CRM systems also focus efforts on developing a plan to provide ongoing technical support that is accessible, visible, and responsive. User support is critical for keeping salespeople on track and instilling confidence in them that there is a "go-to" team in the organization that knows the system and can answer any questions. Many organizations, however, have not perfected their support mechanisms. According Schaaf, just over a third (35 percent) of respondents agreed or strongly agreed that their organization provided good help desk support.

The rollout plan and implementation of sales technologies are only successful if salespeople use the system. While it is critical at this stage that salespeople commit to full adoption, it is at this phase where behavioral change is the most difficult. More CRM systems fail at the execution phase because of poor compliance. There is a resistance by salespeople to report information they learn about the customer because they have always gained prestige by being the sole source of information about the directions their customers might take. In addition, new requirements may be seen by salespeople as an administrative burden. At one company, the most frequently cited reasons for not using the tool included a lack of resources for data entry, "too many inputs required for the outputs we get," a lack of a champion to lead the implementation and manage utilization, a lack of full management support, a fear that "big brother" is watching, and a lack of education or training on how to use the system.

The hesitation of both sharing customer information and taking on additional administrative tasks is a key barrier to sales technology adoption. Organizations successfully implementing sales technologies have taken different approaches, including easing the burden, offering incentives, and implementing mandatory use policies that are tied to performance reviews and compensation. According to one company, "Salespeople are not typically administrators and don't like to be. As a result we use both a carrot approach, by reducing administrative tasks, and a stick, by mandating accurate and timely usage to drive adoption." Organizations that do not incorporate incentives and strict adoption policies typically have greater challenges with usage. For one company in the study, early on, salespeople did not use the system to its potential. According to the company, their CRM system was a "paperweight," as their greatest challenge was "getting salespeople to sync up."

Finally, as mentioned earlier, several organizations in our study either implemented or are in the process of implementing sales technologies on an international basis. Many of the unique challenges with rolling out CRM systems include differences in platform standards, technological sophistication, cultural differences, and infrastructure. Marriott's global CRM system will be designed as a global consolidated inventory system that will allow worldwide tracking of sleeping and meeting rooms. Diebold is implementing a CRM system across all of its foreign operations. While their implementation has been successful, it was not without some challenges, such as technological competency, incompatible technical standards, and cultural issues regarding usage.

BEST PRACTICES AND LESSONS LEARNED (THE FUTURE OF SALES TECHNOLOGIES)

Throughout our research and our discussions with leading organizations, we identified at least three emerging sales technology trends requiring the attention of successful sales organizations:

1. Current and future business challenges will require organizations to adopt flexible and well-thought-out CRM systems.
2. CRM today will only serve to increase customer expectations, requiring organizations to be one step ahead in the race to serve customers and create valuable relationships.
3. Technology is evolving and software systems themselves will be more flexible and sophisticated, requiring organizations to stay on the cutting edge to remain competitive.

The popularity of CRM among organizations we interviewed reflects a fundamental shift to customer-focused strategies and an emphasis on the value of managing mutually beneficial relationships with customers. These companies are taking steps to increase their value to customers and their customers' value to the organization. And as customer relationships become more complex, information becomes more complex.

The challenges to sales organizations discussed throughout this book, including growing global competition, new skill requirements, and new channels to market, will require well-planned and flexible CRM systems if organizations want to strengthen their focus on the customer. For example, as alternative channels and additional customer touch points become more important factors in customer relationships, CRM must take each aspect into account. Additionally, CRM systems also must be fluid and flexible as e-commerce continues to expand and after-sales service becomes more integral to the customer experience.

As customers receive more value from their interactions and continue to have more positive experiences, they will inevitably expect more. For sales organizations to be successful, they will need to meet and exceed those expectations. This will require flawless implementation of CRM systems and the continuous reevaluation of business objectives, sales processes, and individual skills.

Finally, as technologies advance, organizations must be flexible enough to react. Increasingly, CRM systems will not only increase efficiency but effectiveness as well. As current software increases efficiency, for example, by allowing sales reps more time to make sales calls, organizations now also require sales reps to make better and smarter sales calls. Technology providers will focus on making the sales force more effective.

There will be more functionality being put into CRM tools to include knowledge management systems, sales coaching systems, and service intelligence systems. Finally, suppliers of sales force technology will increase their "vertical solutions" and phase out their one-size-fits-all CRM system. Software suppliers now realize that there are different types of customers, business models, and selling strategies, and over time there will be different CRM software to support these differences. Successful sales organizations must be ready to seek out and leverage these technological advances to compete in the global economy.

5

ADOPTING A CONSULTATIVE SELLING APPROACH

"Today I have to listen harder. I no longer 'show up and throw up.' Telling the customer everything I know about my company does not convince them that we are a better supplier. I listen to their goals, their problems, and then work with them to develop a solution to those problems. I am responsible for building trust, for adding value."

—Sales Associate

Another strategy that we heard repeatedly from participant organizations in our study was the adoption of (or a reemphasis on) a consultative selling approach. This is reflective of the salesperson's key role as "being the face" of the organization. As overall corporate strategies and marketing strategies have become more value-based and customer-centric, this philosophy must be represented in each interaction held with customers. As such, a consultative sales approach can be central to creating the desired defining moments with customers. On the surface, this may not seem particularly innovative—after all, most organizations have been talking about consultative selling in some form for at least a decade. What is interesting is that few organizations would claim to have executed on this strategy to the degree sought. In fact, not only are organizations reexamining their use of consultative selling, the approach was held up as the baseline, regardless of industry, geography, or target market. This means that while the transactional sales model will continue to have a place in many sales organizations, it has become a less common use of face-to-face and inside sales channels. What has become the more pressing concern is creating a sales force that understands consultative selling and that can make decisions as to what extent it should be used.

So, what does consultative selling mean and why, after ten years of talking about it, do organizations still think it's worth the considerable effort required? This chapter will explore the answers to these two very important questions.

WHAT IS CONSULTATIVE SELLING?

First, let's define consultative selling. Throughout the course of this study, we heard it referred to by many different names: consultative selling; value-added selling; professional selling; needs satisfaction selling; customer-oriented selling; strategic selling; relationship selling; solution selling; partnering. It is worth noting that each phrase meant something slightly different to the person who used it but, in general, each definition had several of the following key elements in common.

Need-Based Conversations

Within a consultative sales cycle, all sales conversations revolve around a customer need. This is a marked departure from the "product push" approach that still dominates many sales calls today. More specifically, the core of a sales call will be a mutual exchange of information where the salesperson uncovers and develops an understanding of customer needs (or helps the customer become aware of a need). Thus selling becomes a two-way street. To be sure, as one organization notes, "customers may want to buy, but they sure don't want to be sold." Along the same vein, the language the salesperson uses to provide information to the customer should be benefit-oriented—not feature-oriented—and linked to these needs. It's the difference between a digital camera "with 3 megapixels and 3×2 optical

A *New Era of Selling at Honda Clio Shin, Tokyo*

Frequently characterized by aggressive and high-pressure tactics, car sales is perceived as one of the most nonconsultative sales professions left—regardless of what part of the world you live in. Yet even in that highly transactional environment, the need for a more consultative selling approach is gaining significant ground.

Take Honda Clio Shin, one of the largest Honda dealership networks in Japan. As information on products and features becomes so widely available on the Internet, along with purchasing advice and competitive comparisons, Clio found that the average customer was no longer coming to the lot to "collect information" and that their expectations of salespeople had changed.

Faced with this more demanding buyer and an environment of increasing competition, Clio launched the "Committee for Success" project. A critical piece of this initiative is the "with" strategy. The "with" strategy represents a renewed focus on "keeping promises with customers, growing with customers, and working with the local community." Furthermore, Clio renewed its focus on the customer relationships and activity (such as vehicle servicing) that occur post-sale. Among the changes, customers have access to a Web site that assists them with their ongoing vehicle ownership (e.g., directions, troubleshooting, advice, and product knowledge). Furthermore, service transactions are treated as an integral part of the customer relationship as well as an opportunity for sales rather than as a disconnected activity.

Along with this philosophy, of course, comes the need for advanced skills. This new brand of selling was summed up by one respondent, "We can no longer sell without sales skills. Rather we have to listen to the customers' voices carefully to seek out necessary information and identify the car that satisfies those needs—building a reliable relationship with the customer."

zoom" and one that "will allow you to take high-resolution pictures of your upcoming cruise vacation." Both are accurate statements but the latter helps the buyer see how the product will help meet needs. Rocket science? No. But even as the product and service commoditization found in every industry necessitates this transition, you'll find that most sales organizations still spend the majority of its training time and marketing investment on communicating product features instead of benefits.

Multioffering, Creative Solutions

Another key component to this sales approach is the ability of the salesperson to act as a consultant and select products and services from a broad portfolio to create a solution for a client. As a seasoned rep clarified, "I sell projects, not products." This solutions approach presents many challenges as mergers and acquisitions have doubled, even tripled, product sets. As a result, there are cases where it is not realistic for a salesperson to be a product expert in every offering. What typically results is a sales force that is well-versed in some product features, but is not adept at using the information to assemble integrated solutions to meet a client need. Instead, the tendency is to "feature dump," or to rely on recommending only products that they are comfortable with.

The answer, however, does not lie in ramping up product knowledge training. Respondents in our survey indicated a more current view of product knowledge, advocating that the ability to tap in to the product expertise resident in the selling organization (in people or in online systems) has become more important than individual product knowledge itself. Furthermore, according to Wilson (2002), salespeople who are more confident with the skill of selling are more likely to appropriately use product knowledge. This is not to say that product knowledge is not necessary. In fact, Schaaf (2004) found that product knowledge is one of the biggest reasons why purchasers value one

Solutionizing™ at Ingersoll Rand (IR), Taiwan

Traditionally, Ingersoll Rand's Air Solutions division in Taiwan had a customer base comprised of state-owned entities. Today, however, this is changing to a more diversified customer base, including foreign-owned joint ventures. As a result of this change and in support of a new global value proposition called Solutionizing, the sales organization found itself with a need to sell and service in a new way.

Solutionizing promises that IR's Air Solutions will focus on a "customer's energy costs, and increase the reliability, quality, and uptime of compressed air systems." Implicit in this approach is that salespeople will be capable of creating end-to-end systems that solve business problems, such as energy costs, rather than selling the features of an air compressor. As such, salespeople are focused on mastering consultative selling, particularly in regard to playing the role as an advisor or consultant to clients, communicating in benefit language, and becoming more heavily involved in post-sales service activities. As one sales manager noted, "Being an expert in air systems is a lot more than just being able to compare equipment."

salesperson over another. It does imply, however, that product training is better delivered in the context of selling skills, focused on how key features yield valued results and indicative of how the product can be commercially or technically integrated with others in the product suite. This idea was well summed up by a sales training manager, "You can be average with product knowledge—but you will never be great without selling skills."

Unwavering Focus on Value

Another aspect commonly associated with consultative selling was a focus on value. Over time, this has become less of a vague concept around "speaking in benefit language" and much more of a need for being able to articulate quantitative business benefit. Although some of this is clearly due to the impact of a slow economy in recent years, this is no temporary requirement. Increased customer sophistication across the board makes it a mandatory part of the sales cycle. Noted one sales manager, "It's about how to sell value rather than exchanging quotes." Additionally, being able to talk about a solution in terms of ROI (return on investment) or TCO (total cost of ownership) assists in the ability to sell on factors other than just price and in the ability to combat the product and service commoditization that dominates the marketplace.

Speaking ROI at Yellow Book USA

Yellow Book USA, the largest independent yellow pages company, owns and operates more than 600 yellow pages directories in the United States and the United Kingdom. Part of its approach to market is to pursue small business customers. Such businesses include trades, small retail boutiques, restaurants, and medical, financial, and legal practices. Typically, such businesses operate with tight marketing budgets and must carefully scrutinize the return on every expense.

As a result, salespeople must be conversant with regard to the costs and benefits of different media options and be able to express, in financial terms, how a yellow pages advertisement yields results as compared to radio spots or other options. Furthermore, because small business owners (the decision makers) often function as head of sales, marketing, customer service, and more, salespeople must understand and articulate value in terms of the overall business strategy. This means having knowledge of how a variety of different businesses make money along with an understanding of advertising and its role in marketing strategy.

To assist with this daunting task, every sales professional is provided with the training and tools to run ROI calculations and articulate business value in every sales conversation.

The challenge for the salesperson is helping customers understand where value comes from. It may be derived from the benefits of the product or service being sold; it also may come from the ancillary support services or customization that accompany it or the reputation of the supplier organization. Importantly, it may also arise from the information, expertise, and professionalism provided by the salesperson. Being able to articulate value in this manner allows for deeper relationships with customers and, in the business-to-business (B2B) world, at higher levels in the organization.

Aim for Trusted Advisor Status

The last element that was common to each definition was the idea that every salesperson should, in ideal circumstances, aim to become a trusted business advisor to their client base. To be a trusted business advisor with a client means that you have superceded the role of vendor or supplier and are now viewed as an advisor by your clients. To earn such a position with a client, salespeople need to have superior sales skills as well as industry expertise and client insight. Clearly, it might not be practical to invest in this kind of relationship with all clients, nor would all clients desire this kind of relationship with all of their salespeople. Salespeople need to be capable of determining where these relationships are appropriate and they must have the ability to build and maintain them. By providing information and advice as a Trusted Advisor, salespeople are able to add value to the relationship, creating a differentiator versus the competition.

To sum it up, we'll use the following as a working definition for consultative selling:

> Consultative selling is the process of partnering with prospects and customers to create lasting, mutually beneficial relationships. Salespeople who successfully con-

Providing Industry Expertise at Infineum, UK

Infineum is one of world's leading formulators, manufacturers, and marketers of petroleum additives for the fuels and lubricants industry. In addition to the many challenges noted in Chapter 4, Infineum finds itself in the unique situation of operating in an extremely consolidated industry—there are both a limited number of suppliers and of customers. While this environment certainly poses unique challenges, it also provides the opportunity to form deep relationships with every customer.

One of the ways in which Infineum is able to add value and create and maintain these types of relationships is by providing leading-edge industry insight to its customers. This is accomplished through the selection of a very knowledgeable sales force (many of whom are chemists and chemical engineers) and by leveraging an arm of the marketing department, called market managers.

Market managers work as an integral part of the sales team and are responsible for, among many other things, collecting information from markets, countries, manufacturers, industry experts, liaisons, and the like, and compiling it into comprehensive trend analyses. This very valuable output is shared with customers and used to increase the industry expertise of the sales force and distributor network through seminars and briefing notes distributed regularly. This ability to leverage both sales and marketing in business development efforts enables Infineum to improve business results and form tighter relationships with its customers.

struct and build upon these relationships do so by continuously understanding the current and future business issues and needs of the customer and his or her organization, and by providing solutions that provide value helping customers reach their goals. The outcome of this consultative process is for the salesperson to deepen and strengthen the relationship over time, ultimately becoming a trusted business advisor in the customer's eyes.

You'll notice we used the term "working definition." This is because nothing in sales is ever static. Markets change. Customers change. Consultative selling has changed—from referring to any nonaggressive sales approach to the much higher standard outlined above. In the future, the bar will continue to rise.

IT'S BEEN DECADES. WHAT HAPPENED?

During a study of sales organizations conducted in 1986, we constantly heard about the move to consultative selling as the next big frontier for sales professionals. It was therefore somewhat surprising to hear the same strategies expressed some 17 years later. Why has it taken so long to transition from philosophy to standard practice? Just why is consultative selling still the "next big thing"? One reason, of course, relates to the ever-changing nature of sales. Consultative selling means a much higher standard than perhaps envisioned in 1986. Therefore, achieving it has become somewhat like hitting a moving target.

Another reason has to do with timing. Consultative selling takes considerable investment by the supplier. When the market was in a buying mode, as it was in the United States for much of the mid- to late-1990s, anything that lengthened a sales cycle was considered a waste of time. As a result, sales organizations shifted focus and interpersonal selling skills often atrophied in favor of product knowledge and order processing. As the situation began to change and sales cycles became more complex, consultative selling was reintroduced into the mix, at least from a training perspective. Pockets of success were achieved, usually in the areas of national and global account management. However, management reinforcement and a support infrastructure were lacking, and as a result, consultative selling never made the transition from philosophy to consistent, standard practice across sales organizations.

SO WHY BOTHER NOW?

Having established that consultative selling is a skill-, knowledge-, and resource-intensive process, as well as an elusive and moving target, the question becomes, why are organizations still chasing this strategy? The answer lies in the need for long-term perspective. There are different kinds of market conditions that impact sales organizations. Some, such as economic factors, tend to be cyclical and thus short-term in nature. Underlying these is a series of long-term circumstances that, although showcased or masked by cyclical conditions, are by no means temporary.

This is well illustrated by the 2001 recession and the slowdown that followed. Although market challenges, customer demands, and competitive pressures had been growing for a long time, they were somewhat hidden or at least countered by market conditions of economic prosperity. When the cycle reversed, severe budget cutbacks accompanying the economic downturn put the spotlight on these factors. By that time, many organizations were playing catch-up. As a result, the overwhelming feeling among sales organizations today is that the factors that make sales an increasingly complex process are here to stay. Even as economic growth returns, the need to address these challenges will remain. Organizations must be willing to make the investment in consultative selling if they are going to reap the benefits. Noted one top performer, "If you 'go consultant,' you could be adding two to three months to the sales cycle. Of course, you also could be adding all kinds of revenue."

IS CONSULTATIVE SELLING
ALWAYS THE ANSWER?

As noted previously, it may not be practical for all salespeople to practice consultative selling with every customer. The key then, to this new adoption of consultative selling, is a flexible approach that allows a salesperson to determine to what degree to implement it. When, for example, will it make sense for a salesperson to become a Trusted Advisor to a customer? Let's look at this issue using a relationship model. The Sales Impact Ladder in Figure 5.1 shows how different levels of sales behaviors can impact a relationship with a customer. These levels range from transaction-oriented to more consultative in nature.

The first three selling levels describe transactional selling and are characterized by goods and services being exchanged for money. The salesperson's role in these transactions is to facilitate the process and render it painless and even enjoyable, as noted in the following descriptions:

- *Professional Visitor.* This salesperson sells on personality or common interests, often meeting the personal needs of the customer but failing to form a long-term strategic

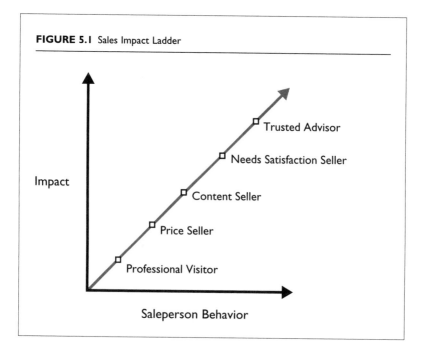

FIGURE 5.1 Sales Impact Ladder

business alliance. Professional Visitors use friendliness and other incentives to get in the door. While it is true that people often buy from people they like, Professional Visitors are unlikely to maximize the potential of an account, because they are rarely viewed as a highly valuable resource.

- *Price Seller.* Conversations in this kind of relationship revolve around price, cost, deals, and quotes. Price Sellers are higher on the ladder than Professional Visitors because they need a bit more knowledge to support negotiations. Price Sellers may meet the customer's financial needs but have difficulty selling the value of a product or service and end up reinforcing a perception of their product or service as a commodity.
- *Content Seller.* This level focuses on product knowledge. Content Sellers typically are highly knowledgeable about their products and try their best to explain it all to customers. The problem is that the sales presentation frequently becomes what is known as a "feature dump"—long on technical information but short on customer benefits.

The two higher consultative levels of the Sales Impact Ladder reflect greater skill and investment but offer more value to customers, support longer-term relationships, and allow for greater salesperson involvement in the buying process. These levels include the following:

- *Needs Satisfaction Seller.* This salesperson uses selling skills to uncover customer needs then tailors the responses. The solutions presented relate directly to the customer's situation and needs. Features are still mentioned, but the emphasis is on the benefit (or value) to the customer. Needs Satisfaction Sellers satisfy the customer's organizational needs by addressing problems and opportunities.
- *Trusted Advisor.* This salesperson has the greatest impact on customers and the sale. It is at this level that the sales-

person's behavior is focused on helping customers succeed in their business. Trusted Advisors are in the strongest
position to form a real business alliance with the customer. They use selling skills to probe at a deeper level—
to discover the business issues that serve as the "need
behind the need" (the reason why the need is important).
Trusted Advisors possess an in-depth understanding of
customer and industry factors and are able to use this expertise to provide value to clients. This kind of relationship
takes significant investment in time and other resources
to create. One example of a sales organization trying to
position itself as an advisor involved executive briefings
on industry topics as the company noted, "We stage free
executive briefings that are all about the customer and not
about sales. We get a good understanding of their top priorities and then build a tailored half-day or full-day briefing where we give them relevant industry information
and noncompetitive examples. Then they know that we
can provide real insight."

A salesperson can be successful at every stage of the ladder.
Clearly, the Needs Satisfaction Seller and the Trusted Advisor
would be preferred by most selling organizations because they
are most resistant to client turnover. This is not always feasible,
however, and the dilemma becomes knowing where on the ladder you should be with any given client. There are two key
questions to ask: "What kind of relationship does this client desire from a supplier?" and "What makes good business sense?"

WHAT DO CUSTOMERS WANT?

Let's start with the customer perspective. Decision making
generally covers six major stages:

1. *Plan and prioritize.* This involves determining the organizational goals and objectives and outlining the actions needed to achieve them. During this process, customers will uncover barriers, issues, and challenges that must be addressed in order to succeed.
2. *Identify options.* At this point, the question becomes: "What are my options to overcome this challenge?" During this phase of the process, customers are concerned with make/buy decisions and identifying supplier candidates.
3. *Evaluate options.* This stage involves narrowing the supplier universe down to a select few, often using formal criteria.
4. *Select the best option.* At this point, possibilities are further narrowed down to one alternative.
5. *Contract.* Here the parties agree on how to work together (often includes negotiations around terms and conditions, such as price, durations, and service level requirements).
6. *Build and track.* This level involves the ongoing implementation, use, and maintenance of the solution.

Customers may find value in having salespeople participate in all of these phases or they may find value in only limited participation. For example, if a customer is already in the "evaluate options" stage, then a lower-ladder or transactional approach may be most appropriate. On the other hand, if the client is open to salesperson involvement throughout a broader portion of the process, then a more consultative approach may be appropriate. For example, a customer may value the efforts of a Needs Satisfaction Seller to assist in drilling down into problems and identifying options to address those problems. When a customer values involvement in all stages of the process, from business planning to post-sales use, it becomes possible for a salesperson to achieve Trusted Advisor status. Figure 5.2 shows how different rungs of the ladder align with a customer's decision-making process.

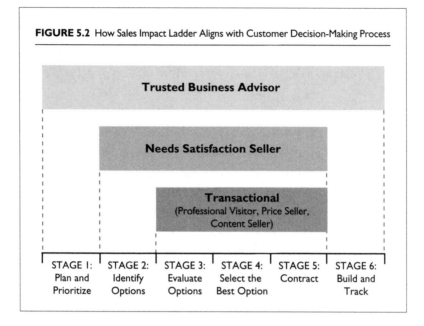

FIGURE 5.2 How Sales Impact Ladder Aligns with Customer Decision-Making Process

BALANCING CUSTOMER POTENTIAL AND COST OF SALES

At the same time, a salesperson has to take into account what their *internal* customers are looking for. Customers who may be looking for a salesperson to advise their decisions throughout the phases may only represent a very small opportunity for the business. In such cases, it may make sense for the salesperson to look for ways to more efficiently deliver value (e.g., delivering newsletters as opposed to in-depth financial reviews) to the client without overinvesting their limited resources.

When we looked across the organizations in our study, we found that, in general, transactional customers were served by inside sales teams and distributor networks or were given incentives to use self-service channels, such as e-commerce. Face-to-face sales teams, as well as some groups of inside sales resources, were reserved for customers with whom a consultative relationship was desired. The goal in these instances was to preserve the investment in a direct sales force for those segments and opportunities that had the highest potential. That is not to say that face-to-face sales teams never engaged in transactional sales or that inside sales resources could not have consultative relationships with clients. Just the opposite may occur, depending on what the buyer and seller are looking for in the relationship. But in general, the highest valued resources were deployed for those customers who valued a consultative approach and who were considered key to the selling organization.

CAN A CUSTOMER MOVE UP THE RELATIONSHIP LADDER?

Relationships may vary along the ladder. Salespeople may find themselves in different stages depending on the opportunity and the decision maker in an account (e.g., the business manager may view the salesperson as a Needs Satisfaction Seller while the procurement manager may view that person as a Price Seller). In general, however, it is rare for a client to grow a relationship from one that is highly transactional to one that is highly consultative. More commonly, if the progression occurs, it is gradual and the salesperson's requirements will shift as well. Research conducted by Beverland (2001) indicates that as relationships with clients grow, the balance of relationship-based (understanding client industry) and performance-based (closing sales calls) activities will shift toward the latter.

Caution should be exercised here, however. Clients may grow their relationship with you if you exceed performance expectations or perhaps if they are considering entering a new market in which your company has expertise. However, they may be content to maintain their status quo at a lower end of the ladder. Even if a customer is very large, they may forever view your relationship as transactional and you may never be able to move up the ladder with them to earn more than minimal revenues. In these cases, it makes sense to control the investment in sales instead of chasing the "big elephant"—even considering passing the opportunity to a channel with a lower cost of sale, such as an inside salesperson who will be able to meet client relationship expectations with less investment. On the other hand, it may make sense for an inside sales representative to hand off an account to a face-to-face sales team if the client prefers a deeper relationship and the account potential merits a higher cost of sale.

BEST PRACTICES AND LESSONS LEARNED

The focus of every sales organization we talked to was to fight off commoditization and meet the needs of an increasingly sophisticated customer base by leveraging a consultative selling approach executed through the face-to-face and (upon occasion) inside sales forces. This was true regardless of the sales model (business-to-business, business-to-consumer), solution set (e.g., cell phones, large outsourcing solutions), or industry (e.g., telecommunications, financial services, manufacturing). The key to success in each case was ensuring that the right resources have the right capabilities to execute on the right relationships. This may mean learning to look for ways to progress an account up the Sales Impact Ladder, being flexible enough to scale down a consultative approach for a less involved client, or even handing off a consultative opportunity to a different channel.

Our experiences working with clients who have embarked on this journey to consultative selling has yielded some critical success factors. These can be summarized by three major themes:

1. Use a holistic approach.
2. Put everything in the context of a formal sales process.
3. Make sure you have the support infrastructure in place.

A consistent success factor throughout our organizational studies has been the presence of a holistic approach. This starts with an executive vision and cascades throughout the organization—from managerial reinforcement down to consistent field execution. When asked why consultative selling had been so slow to achieve its potential, the majority of answers we got indicated a fragmented message to the sales force: managers weren't modeling consultative selling skills; different segments of the sales and service organizations were trained on differing skills and philosophy. Therefore, to truly expect any results from adopting a consultative selling approach, organizations need to view it as a strategic initiative—enlisting the necessary resources and conveying the essential communication across the organization to make it successful. Sometimes, the consultative philosophy lacks reinforcement in the field, other times it can even be directly contradicted. As one organization offered, "We had one sales manager, and after his people would come back from training, he would send them out to a used car dealership for three days—to show them how it's really done!"

Another point worth making is that a consultative sales approach should not be isolated within the sales organization. Customers deal with organizations through a number of contact points: marketing, customer service, and fulfillment, for example. Customer experiences throughout the relationship should be similar, whether they are dealing with their relationship manager or someone who is installing purchased equipment or researching an account transaction.

Once the philosophy is communicated across the organization, it must become actionable. For salespeople, this means that consultative selling must be part of their daily sales interactions; it must be embedded in a formally defined sales process. Although such processes will vary by organization, Figure 5.3 represents a typical example.

Defining a sales process is a complex project involving a cross-functional team comprised of marketing managers, sales-

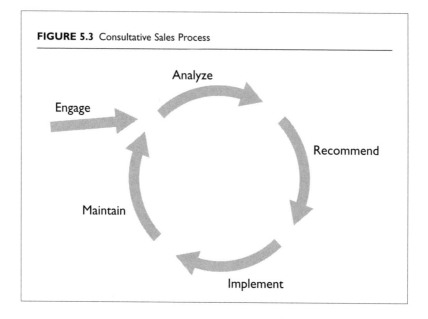

FIGURE 5.3 Consultative Sales Process

people, customer service representatives, operations, and customers themselves. Once assembled, this team analyzes customer touch points and determines the desired process for creating and maintaining customer relationships. While defining this process represents a huge milestone, the real value becomes defining the detail that supports it. Every phase must become actionable by defining what the customer expectations are, what the sales activities are, and how success will be measured. (See Figure 5.4.) From this, a salesperson is able to understand how consultative selling behaviors link to what he or she does for a living and how they assist in creating relationships with clients.

Perhaps the biggest temptation to overcome in these situations is what is known as "analysis paralysis." This means collecting so much data and conducting so much planning that the output is not actionable. Make sure to look at things in manageable pieces. For example, create parameters for the sales process—map out a process that starts when a prospect is first

FIGURE 5.4 Dissecting the Analyze Phase

Customer Expectations	• Ask me questions that are relevant. • Don't waste my time. • Do your homework. • Help me think through my needs. • Listen to what I have to say.
Key Activities	• Create a probing strategy based on researching the customer's situation. • Listen carefully and confirm your understanding. • Ask questions to gain a clear, complete, and mutual understanding of a customer's needs.
Measurement	• Customer should find value in analysis phase (customer satisfaction survey). • Salesperson should ask appropriate questions to develop clear, complete, and mutual understanding (coaching observation).

received as a lead and ends with post-sales activities conducted by the sales force (instead of extending into customer service or implementation activities).

Even if you have a holistic vision and an integrated sales process, you will need to enable execution through a support infrastructure.

In our observations, the biggest pitfall is when a disconnect between desired sales behavior and actual sales behavior occurs because of misalignment with the compensation and incentive system. All too frequently, we will work with sales organizations who are frustrated with the lack of consultative selling they witness in the field. Further investigation reveals that salespeople are being tasked with a consultative selling approach but being compensated for transactional behaviors. For example, a salesperson for a midsized services firm admitted, "I have a monthly quota. I may accept longer sales cycles at the beginning of the month, but when the end of the month comes around I give up on selling solutions—I'm back to selling units [of hardware]."

Therefore, once that sales process is developed, organizations need to take a step back and do a gap analysis. What is the difference between this process and the way selling occurs today? What needs to change? What support is needed? And of course, never forget to pay people for what you want them to do. As one organization confessed, "We want our salespeople to be better businesspeople and are looking at compensation based on profitability. Today, it's based on booked revenue; previously, it only was based on order amounts."

RESKILLING
THE SALES FORCE

"When you had a sales force that was successful in selling [a specific line of products], moving them to solution sales was difficult. We had to go significantly revamp the sales force."

—Sales Director

Many, if not all, of the strategies in this book will require organizations to rethink the kinds of skills that are required for their salespeople and managers. In fact, many organizations are undertaking a "reskilling" of the sales force as a distinct strategy for overcoming the challenges in the current and future selling environment. This reskilling involves determining the desired salesperson profile and integrating it into selection and performance management, as well as into training and development systems.

COMPETENCIES DEFINE SALES SUPERSTARS

Over the years, we have had the opportunity to conduct many studies in the area of selling skills. These competency studies are conducted using a critical incident methodology in which patterns of behaviors, skills, and attributes are extracted from anecdotal descriptions. In layman's terms, this means that when you ask a salesperson why he or she is successful, it is hard for that salesperson to articulate the reasons. But, if you talk to many salespeople and ask them to describe what they did in both successful and unsuccessful selling situations, you'll find commonalties that indicate the presence of selling competencies. In our most recent competency study (Del Gaizo, 2001), we collected over 2,000 of these anecdotes or critical incidents and used them to identify which competencies were linked to successful sales. To have the competencies be more actionable, we grouped them into roles that a salesperson must fulfill. We found five such roles:

1. Long-Term Ally
2. Business Consultant
3. Strategic Orchestrator
4. Consistent Cultivator
5. Focused Optimist

When we conducted our most recent research study into sales strategies, we wanted to know how sales leaders thought these sales skills might change in the future—What new skills would be required? What would the next generation of sales superstars look like?

We did not, however, uncover any evidence of "new" roles during this project. What we found was that the roles themselves were the same, but the bar had been raised and expectations for each were much higher than they had been in the past. As with many other strategies in our study, there was no longer any room for philosophical buy-in, the next frontier was consistent execution. A brief discussion of the five roles follows, along with an indication of how organizations in our study are focusing on each to gain an advantage in the marketplace.

The Long-Term Ally

As noted by Keilor (2000), salesperson revenue is correlated to what are considered to be the relational aspects of selling, most notably having a "customer orientation" as opposed to a "selling orientation." This means uncovering and serving client needs with a *long-term* perspective. This is reflected within the role termed the Long-Term Ally, which is focused on the interpersonal aspect of selling and of conveying a sense of shared purpose with the customer. To be perceived as a long-term partner to a client, salespeople must be able to develop long-term client relationships, facilitate open and continuous communications, and act as a customer advocate within their own organization. Skills within the Long-Term Ally role were most frequently mentioned by study participants as being critical to future success. Their focus was on the changing definition of "relationships" and the increasing implications of "long term."

First, there were few if any interviews where the concept of relationship selling did not come up. Without such relationships, transactions become commodity-based: "The Internet is working against us. Open markets are working against us." It's short-term gain and long-term loss when relationships are out of the picture. In many cases, these relationships were changing from being personal in nature to being more often characterized as professional. Time and time again we heard that "in the end, it is all about relationships." While there will always be some truth to the statement "People prefer to buy from those they like," it appears to be much less of a factor than it used to be. In fact, buyers indicate that a salesperson's "friendliness" is less influential over purchase decisions than their ability to be "trusted" (see Chapter 9).

The difference is subtle, but mentioned repeatedly throughout our conversations. As one salesperson in our study noted, "We're moving from personal relationships to strategic account management." This does not mean that personality attributes are no longer important. What it does mean is that salespeople must be more knowledgeable and must be able to provide more value to the customer then just being enjoyable to be around. This has been particularly significant in business-to-business (B2B) selling relationships. As B2B buyer processes now fre-

A *New Generation of Relationship Selling at Diebold*

Diebold is a manufacturer of automatic teller machines (ATMs), electronic and physical security systems, and election systems. Its core customer base (for the ATM and security lines of business) lies largely in the banking industry. The sales approach used in the banking industry has historically been "relationship selling," meaning "building long-term, rapport-based relationships with branch bank operations personnel." Now, however, as banks consolidate and move to centralized procurement (often using third-party consultants), many of those relationships have disappeared. As one longtime sales representative summed it up, "It's more difficult to socialize with clients. Now it's all about whoever gives a better price."

To compete, Diebold had to move relationship selling to a new level. Relationships are clearly still vital to success, but they are now more business driven, built by consultative selling skills rather than rapport. In this environment, sales professionals must find decision makers and build relationships— before requests for proposals (RFPs) get created. To do so requires more prep work, a continuous presence in front of a client, and a higher level of industry knowledge. It also means holding sales conversations with a wide variety of decision makers concentrating on a wide variety of business issues, including increased revenues, increased customer satisfaction, and reduced opportunity costs. For example, this might mean that instead of talking about "ATM speeds and feeds," a salesperson would have to talk about "multichannel delivery strategies, teller compensation issues, and the like. That way you can provide real value to the customer."

quently include decision-making committees or procurement, personal ties between organizations are often broken. The extent to which this happens also depends on cultural differences. In Latin America, the character of B2B selling is still most often viewed as a personal event where face-to-face engagements, building rapport, and social interaction are considered to be paramount to selling success. In parts of Asia, personal relationships, although viewed as separate, are considered a necessary precursor to professional relationships. In all cases, though, salespeople are under increased pressure to provide value beyond just the personal aspects of the relationship.

The other main focus with regard to the Long-Term Ally role was a bigger-picture perspective on what "long term" meant. The result was a greater focus on post-sales activities to maintain relationships over the longer term. Salespeople were increasingly getting involved in servicing or implementation activity and were much more engaged in post-sales transactions for account maintenance. This focus on lifetime client value was true of business-to-consumer (B2C) situations as well. Even in a transactional retail environment, a long-term perspective is desired. Although it is unlikely in some B2C transactions that the customer will ever deal with any salesperson more than once, they will have a long-term relationship with the brand that should be supported through the discrete transactions with salespeople. As such, interacting with customers as part of a long-term relationship is viewed as a goal of industries of all types.

The Business Consultant

The term *Business Consultant* is used to describe the role in which a salesperson leverages reputation, product knowledge, industry expertise, and customer insight to provide value to their customer as a consultant and partner rather than just as a vendor. On a more tactical level, being a Business Consultant requires mastery of consultative selling techniques, such as being able to assemble relevant solutions and present, propose, and close sales. The key is that increasingly organizations are trying to elevate their relationships with buyers and buying organizations, which calls for being able to sell to C-level executives. This holds true in the B2C marketplace as well. The goal of a more consultant-like relationship calls for being able to sell value at different levels and address different layers of need.

If we think about one of the strategies discussed previously, "Adopting a Consultative Selling Approach," it is clear that being able to fulfill the role of the Business Consultant will be critical for organizations taking a more consultative approach. At the same time, it's certain that being a Business Consultant has become more and more difficult as customers have become more sophisticated. Difficult as it may be, being a Business Consultant is still a desired space for most sales organizations that view it as a real differentiator in the market. As one sales manager noted, "Our approach used to be about as strategic as a paperclip but now we try to help businesses integrate the way they do business, reduce their costs, and help them improve productivity." To successfully execute on such a tall order, salespeople need to be more skilled at selling on value as well as on selling to higher-level executives. Further, they have to have a solid knowledge base that includes business/industry knowledge, product knowledge, financial acumen, and customer insight. One sales leader noted the challenge in achieving this level of expertise, "The 90s were a wild successful curve, but looking underneath, the sales organization had lost a lot of what had set the company up for success to begin with—a fundamental understanding of key vertical markets. We lost our understanding of the customer's environment."

It should be noted that although a solid product knowledge base is critical in providing the credibility needed to be viewed as a Business Consultant, it does not necessarily mean that all

Participating in the Client Value Chain at Infineon

Infineon Technologies is a German-based company offering semiconductor solutions from pure hardware components over chipsets and software solutions up to complete reference platforms and service consultancy for a wide range of applications. Over time, Infineon has reduced its customer base and put more focus on selected accounts. For the direct sales force at Infineon, this means that "there are fewer customers to call on, but calls are more intense and the sales process becomes more complex." As a result, Infineon's sales force is required to "understand more about the market, supply chain management, and the customer's business models." By understanding how their clients' businesses operate, Infineon's sales professionals aim to form deeper, more valuable relationships with customers—to "add value in terms of complex consulting"—and differentiate themselves in the marketplace.

salespeople should be product experts. In fact, many of the organizations we spoke with were moving to a model where salespeople were considered product "generalists." They were expected to be able to discuss the entire breadth of products, at a high level, leveraging product specialists when more detail was required. This often was used when the solutions being sold were highly technical in nature. Having account executives operate as generalists encourages solution instead of product sales, and can promote a focus on relationships instead of transactions. Furthermore, this allows for more pinpointed and strategic use of product specialists who can be invaluable in closing sales. As one information technology (IT) sales manager noted, "The more specialists you have, the more sales you can generate."

The Strategic Orchestrator

When a salesperson acts as a Strategic Orchestrator, they are focused on creating connections between and within the selling and buying entities in order to manage the sales process, expedite a sale, encourage the exchange of information, and make it easy for the customer to deal with the selling organization. At one company, this was referred to as "coordinative selling." As with the other roles discussed, this had become more challenging as customers' needs became more complex, selling entities became larger, and customers began to favor "arm's-length" buying processes.

The Strategic Orchestrator role has become increasingly more important to organizations. Of particular focus is the need to utilize influencing skills to leverage internal resources. As one organization noted, "You need to ask yourself the question: 'How do I get other people to work for me and with me even if they don't report to me?'" We also frequently heard organizations talk about the need for salespeople to become better resource managers. As one sales manager noted, "It's about team selling and using the operational excellence of the busi-

---

Internal Selling at Infineum

At Infineum, internal selling skills are viewed as just as important to success as external selling skills. To succeed in their marketplace, sales professionals are increasingly asked to act as "resource managers" or "strategic facilitators" in order to bring the organization's assets to the benefit of a specific client or project. Infineum sales directors see this as "less about selling skills and more on how you get other people to work for you and with you." By mastering such influencing skills and becoming better Strategic Orchestrators, Infineum sales professionals are better able to manage virtual team constructs and act as advocates for their accounts.

ness. The salesperson needs to pull all of the right levers in order to bring in the right resources." This can be challenging as organizations merge and grow to include more complex organizational structures comprised of greater numbers of teams, channels, and resources. However, it is absolutely necessary if organizations are to take best advantage of the matrixed sales organizations (discussed in Chapter 3).

The Consistent Cultivator

This Consistent Cultivator role is all about the salesperson's ability to plan and manage the totality of their accounts. Salespeople who are successful at this role are those who proactively manage time and territory and who are diligent in maintaining and expanding their presence in accounts. Given today's emphasis on new business acquisition (and the mature position of many of the industries in our study), organizations seemed most concerned with doing a better job at mining new business opportunities with current accounts. As a director of sales noted, "We want to have our [global account representatives] work as successfully when they penetrate an organization vertically as they do when they work horizontally." For the B2B world, this might mean uncovering new buying centers, for B2C it could mean actively exploring new areas of need. As another organization noted, "I don't want our people to just sit there [on the retail floor] and wait to be approached. I want them to be proactive, be proposing, be selling."

As selling approaches become more consultative in nature, this can become more challenging. As an example, Krishnamurthy (2003) takes special note of the circumstances that surround solution selling (assembling unique solutions for individual customer needs as opposed to product sales). In its estimation, an account team that utilizes a solution selling model will have to call on three to four times as many people

Elevating Account Management Skills at Hewlett Packard

As the new postmerger HP has emerged, the focus for the sales organization has been to form deeper relationships with customers—"to sell the value and business benefits of the entire portfolio." In forming and managing these account relationships, HP relies on a consistent sales process across its major B2B selling organizations. Using a consistent process helps salespeople better penetrate an organization vertically as well as horizontally "being able to dive into the different business divisions, understand the variety of business drivers and challenges, and to explain to each how technology can help them meet those challenges."

Superior account management skills are expected to help salespeople become consultants in the eyes of their executive level clients, earning "a seat at the strategy table" and uncovering more opportunities to leverage their new breadth and depth of solutions.

in different functions and business units at a single customer than they would for a product sale.

Another trend among organizations with regard to the Consistent Cultivator is a more strategic approach to territory management. Agreed one sales trainer, "We are definitely moving from an opportunistic approach to a planned approach for territory management." During cycles of economic prosperity, or in cases where technology firms were able to secure longer-term, first-mover advantages, salespeople often were able to fill their pipeline just by answering the phone when it rang. Now, however, such windows of opportunity are often narrower. Therefore, a more proactive approach to prospecting and pipeline management is required. Sales organizations are utilizing technology tools, support resources, and research services to support opportunity qualification and help salespeople be more effective. However, the most important shift is a mind-set change whereby salespeople are expected to be able to understand an organization's sales strategy and apply it to their own territories. Who should they be spending the most time with? Where will the biggest opportunities be found? How can they leverage corporate and marketing messages to the marketplace? In this sense then, salespeople are becoming more like business managers of a territory instead of taking a more reactive, activity-based approach to territory management.

The Focused Optimist

If organizations were spending the majority of their time thinking about being Business Consultants and Long-Term Allies, they were spending the least amount of their time worried about being Focused Optimists. This role is all about what top performers do to create a positive atmosphere that makes selling an enjoyable and frequent activity for sellers and buyers alike. A combination of persistence and an ability to maintain a sense of optimism keeps them moving forward and causes others to want to work with them. Salespeople successful at this role are motivated to succeed, are able to get and keep the attention of clients and stakeholders, and they meet their commitments to both. As one manager explains, "We want people who, in severe conditions, can think 'I can make it' as opposed to 'this situation is just too hard.'"

What is interesting about this role is that it hardly ever came up in interviews. While a slowdown in the economy may have reemphasized the need for optimism, there was nothing to indicate that this role would be executed any differently going forward than it is today. We interpret this not as a disinterest in the attitudes and personalities of salespeople, but instead as an indication that being a Focused Optimist simply "went without saying."

B*uilding PIT Crews at Bell South*

Bell South's small business division faces several very challenging conditions in its business environment: competition has exploded in a deregulated market, while at the same time, new federal regulations have restricted offerings and pricing models; and customer expectations have increased exponentially. "It used to be that customers were just happy if they picked up the phone and had a dial tone. Now they are concerned about other issues like wireless capabilities, disaster recovery systems, and more."

It takes a highly motivated sales representative to succeed in this environment. Bell South has looked at its sales force to determine the model for salesperson success. This model for successful sales associates has been dubbed the PIT Crew, which stands for *P*assionate people, *I*nspirational leaders, and *T*echnical heroes. Such salespeople are "persistent, willing to learn the customer's business and sell solutions, willing to spend more time preparing for sales calls, and able to execute a deeper level of consultative selling."

There also was an increased focus on emotional intelligence, which we noted as we heard more on the idea of salespeople being able to utilize personality traits and conveyance of attitudes. Emotional intelligence, or EI, is a type of social intelligence that involves "the ability to perceive and monitor one's own and others' emotions, to discriminate among them, understand the information of those emotions, and to use the information to guide one's thinking and actions" (Mayer and Salovey, 1993). Emotional intelligence suggests that once individuals recognize the meaning of emotions and their relationships, they are then able to reason based on them. Daniel Goleman, in his 1995 book *Emotional Intelligence: Why It Can Matter More than IQ,* is more widely credited with popularizing the term *EI.* Goleman's book discusses in detail the five domains of EI (self-awareness, managing emotions, handling feelings, motivating oneself, and empathy). Goleman goes on to apply the concept of EI to the corporate world using the key concepts of self-mastery and relationship skills. Several organizations in our study were looking at the topic with greater interest and trying to determine whether it was useful as a selection, awareness, or training and development tool for selling resources.

The idea of having a personality for selling persists in organizations today. A salesperson's enthusiasm about the selling role clearly transfers to clients and prospects as "I love this job. I believe in this product."

THE IMPORTANCE OF SELECTION

Any major change in the sales organization may require a new kind of sales resource to deliver on it. Sometimes this is achieved through upgrading the skills of the current sales teams. In other cases, a more dramatic restructuring is undertaken. Krishnamurthy (2002) indicates that large-scale changes, such as a move to solution selling, could require an organization to replace more than 50 percent of its existing product sales force within the first 12 months. In fact, they estimate less than a third of a product-oriented sales team will be able to make the leap to solution sales. Given the constant change referred to throughout this text and the magnitude of it, it is not surprising that there is a continuous focus on finding talent within all of the sales organizations we spoke with. Even in recent times when job seekers were in great supply, being able to properly support strategies with qualified resources was never far from the minds of sales leaders. Noted one, "One thing we've got to work on is making sure that our people don't get poached by the competition. It's always a possibility, always a worry."

Combining the fact that sales is traditionally a high turnover function with a view of the significant investment required to recruit, it is clearly critical to reduce the risk in hiring decisions and earn a better return on personnel investments. As such, a strategic approach to salesperson selection is a must.

Selection methods vary by organization. There is no one way that has been scientifically proven to guarantee or come close to ensuring a successful hire. Primarily, organizations will utilize personal interviewing in combination with other methods to make decisions about whether to bring someone into the sales organization. In fact, Randall (2001) includes interviewing, biodata collection, assessment centers, recommendation letters, reference checks, handwriting analysis, personality testing, and even blood type inferences among methods used today. Because there is no clear-cut best practice, the magic then is not in any particular selection methodology but in ensuring that it is tied to a clear set of competencies and job profiles. Are you hiring people who are or can be Business Consultants? Are you prepared to help them make the journey? As one sales manager lamented, "For years we hired the wrong people and wasted time trying to coach and develop people who couldn't be developed." More succinctly put by another manager, "Put an idiot in training and get a trained idiot."

TRAINING TO DEVELOP NEW SKILL SETS

In addition, many organizations will approach an initiative to reskill the sales force by instituting formal training and development functions. At present though, The American Society of Training and Development (ASTD) estimates that only 39 percent of U.S. companies provide sales training to their selling organizations. Even then, training often is focused on product knowledge—even at the expense of selling skills and sales processes. While product knowledge is certainly a critical element of selling, it can be costly to use it as a replacement for interpersonal skills, financial acumen, or other needed competencies. In fact, in a study of training effectiveness, Dubinsky

(1996) indicated that a greater proportion of product knowledge did not increase the impact of sales training.

The organizations in our study took a variety of approaches to sales training—some had integrated curricula while others did spot training on an ad hoc basis; some focused on supporting ongoing skill development while others concentrated mainly on new hires; some delivered exclusively product knowledge training while others delivered a variety of product knowledge, interpersonal skills, and technical training.

Ideally, organizations are moving toward an integrated, ongoing, multilayered curriculum. However, given the environment in which salespeople operate, creating a learning and development culture—much less executing a single training initiative—can be quite challenging. Sales training needs to provide value greater than the opportunity costs of being out of the field, in addition to delivery and personnel costs. It should be implemented to address a varied audience, often geographically dispersed and with a variety of backgrounds and learning styles. Furthermore, it should concentrate on skills and processes that can be immediately applied in the field, facilitated by someone who has sales experience. Anything that is perceived as being academic or too theoretical will never live beyond the classroom (or the Web module). As Wilson (2002) notes, if training content and selling environment are misaligned or disconnected, the ability to transfer training to on-the-job performance improvement will suffer significantly.

Even meeting all of these requirements won't ensure success. If we look at interpersonal skills or sales processes as an example (like the competencies mentioned in this chapter), a structured approach is required. In fact, our experience has shown that to increase the likelihood of behavior change, a learner needs to go through the following series of five phases that occur before, during, and after what is traditionally considered "training":

1. *Commit to learn.* Learners must open themselves to new possibilities and resolve to master and apply essential skills. This is facilitated through program elements, such as prework and opening exercises, that help participants understand how skill and behavior changes could benefit them.

2. *Assess current performance.* Recognizing and monitoring performance gaps motivates learners and helps them focus their efforts. This gap analysis can be accomplished through manager observations or self-observations and by utilizing the assessment and measurement tools incorporated into your organization's training programs.

3. *Acquire knowledge.* Within the training program itself, a varierty of methods and tools (video, reading, dicussion, observation, analysis, etc.) are used to assist the learner in acquiring knowledge and understanding specific skills.

4. *Develop competency through practice.* If knowledge is skills-based, then it has to be practiced. This can include practicing technical skills (e.g., flight simulators). The training of interpersonal skills on the other hand (e.g., selling skills) requires practicing live with humans. This can take place within the training programs themselves or during live follow-up sessions (face-to-face or by using teleconference or synchronous Web capabilities).

5. *Apply new training.* A range of application and reinforcement tools—peer- and manager-led discussions, planners, and job aids—can be used to give learners the clarity needed to apply skills to real-life situations. Further, managers of learners can reinforce and sustain skill and knowledge application through coaching, recognition of use, and consistent modeling in their own interactions.

For example, a sales training intervention regarding account management might look something like Figure 6.1.

FIGURE 6.1 How a Learner Might Move through the Learning Formula Phases

Commit	• Receive e-mail from sales director indicating purpose and value of training.
	• Have discussion with manager to explore how training might assist with current account situations.
	• Complete "prework" before training that asks for reflection on how training might be beneficial and what the expectations from the training and trainer are.
Assess	• Complete self-assessment (and/or ask a current client to complete an evaluation of your account management skills).
	• Have coaching session with manager to review skill gaps and identify where to focus efforts during upcoming training.
	• Make plans for and execute post-training assessment and evaluation.
Acquire	• Attend training (classroom or Web) and learn new skills and processes for how to analyze accounts and develop short-term as well as long-term account strategies.
Develop	• Practice newly learned skills and processes in a safe environment (within training intervention or with peer group) using examples or actual account data. Make sure to focus on areas identified as gaps during pretraining assessment.
	• Receive and incorporate feedback from other training participants and session facilitator.
Apply	• Use reinforcement tools and job aids to apply the new account management process to all major accounts in your territory.
	• Review account planners, skills, and processes in coaching sessions.
	• Attend follow-up practice and application sessions held by manager.

As you can see, there is clearly much more to development than just sending a salesperson to a class or providing access to a Web module. However, most organizations approach learning and development in a fragmented manner—leadership training is conducted by Human Resources, sales skills training by the sales or marketing departments, product knowledge training by the Marketing department or from vendors, and technical training from yet another functional area. As a result, most focus is spent on the Acquire and Develop phases, while little is spent on the rest. In fact, a recent survey of 300 sales executives (Galea 2002) reported that over half (57 percent) indicated that they were not aware of measurement systems associated with training in their organizations.

BEST PRACTICES AND LESSONS LEARNED

When it comes to reskilling the sales force, a strategic approach is required, starting with an overarching vision and ending up with integration and alignment among selection, training and development, performance management, competency assessment, compensation, and other human resources systems. The following is a best practice process for how such change can be enacted. Many of the organizations in our study were reexamining their competency models and job profiles in such a manner in order to achieve a new level of selling ability in the fields.

Agree on what kinds of relationships you are trying to form with customers. The first step is to take a step back. Selling organizations need to determine what kinds of relationships they are trying to create and with what kinds of clients. This involves formally identifying and documenting the sales process for each target audience. Although it may sound simple, creating a sales process is an important activity that involves many parts of the organization—sales, marketing, and customer service, along with customers themselves. Once you have agreed on how relationships should be created with customers, you can break down the process into the following phases:

- *Engage.* This is the first interaction with the customer to qualify the customer as a prospect (or an opportunity) and gain an initial appointment.

- *Analyze.* This step involves needs analysis; ask questions to understand the customer's situation.
- *Recommend.* Here you propose an appropriate solution based on the information collected.
- *Implement.* At this stage, you get acceptance and implement the solution for the customer.
- *Maintain.* Here you continue to build the customer relationship postsale.

Determine what kinds of resources you will need to form this relationship. After you have identified the sales process and broken it in to discrete phases, you should go back and think about what kinds of resources would be required to create the desired relationships. In some cases, it may make the most sense to have one type of resource assigned to manage the entire process. For example, you might find that a key account manager might be necessary for all of the phases when building relationships with large global accounts. In other cases, relationships might best be constructed and managed using multiple resources. For example, if we use the above process as a guide, an inside sales group could manage the engage phase, a territory rep for the analyze, recommend, and implement phases, and a dedicated inside salesperson for the maintain phase.

Identify the competencies (skills, knowledge, and attributes) needed in each phase of the sales process for each job profile. With the resources identified, it's time to create job profiles for each. This will be based on an analysis of the sales process— what each resource should be doing at each phase of the process, and what characteristics will lead to success. Identifying competencies can be an involved process. Often it is accomplished through detailed studies whereby the top and bottom performing tiers of a sales force are observed and tested. Comparing the backgrounds, skills, attributes, and behaviors of the two groups and correlating the differences to a differential in success leads to an identification of key competencies. Some-times, organizations are able to use general competency mod-els (such as the Salesperson Competency Assessment found in Appendix B) that are derived from multi-industry studies and observations. For example, if we think about the salesperson who handles the engage phase of the sales process above, that individual should be:

- Knowledgeable of how to conduct precall research
- Able to prioritize prospecting activities based on the sales strategy
- Able to initiate conversations with customers
- Adept at keeping customer's attention during conversations
- Able to successfully close calls by making appointments
- Able to convey familiarity with common industry issues
- Persistent and resilient
- Able to use clear and concise communication skills (par-ticularly over the phone)

Develop a view of competency progression. Once the com-petencies have been identified, it becomes important to look at them as a set. Which are more advanced than the others? How might individuals progress from one job profile to another? Are there needs for levels within the job profiles (e.g., account executive, senior account executive, etc.)? This helps facilitate the use of the profiles for career planning and selection and helps determine the sequencing of development activities in an integrated curriculum.

Integrate job profiles and skill requirements into performance management activities. In order for people to move among roles in the sales organization, they will need to be able to assess their own abilities against those required in the job profile. This is done in a collaborative manner between a salesperson and the sales manager, including ongoing coaching sessions as well as regular performance reviews. Unfortunately, performance management is not always linked with job profiles and as a result becomes more of a paper-pushing exercise than a development activity. In fact, in *CLO Magazine,* Brennan (2004) recently conducted a study into the character of performance management activities that pointed out that although almost every respondent (99 percent) indicated that their organization used performance reviews, 61 percent said that such reviews "do not really influence the training and development that employers offer." Further, the study indicated that only slightly more than half (55 percent) of respondents felt like their performance management system "integrates organizational goals, individual competencies, and ongoing employee development plans."

Cascade job profiles into training and development functions. Training and development activity should be linked directly to the competencies and job profiles identified as necessary for executing the sales strategy. Full curricula can be created that are aimed specifically at improving the sales force's ability to deliver on its role in creating relationships. As individuals are coached by their managers, they will then be able to determine, on an individual basis, which training activities might be the most beneficial in helping them improve performance in their role. Further, they can determine which programs might help them become better suited for other job profiles.

Integrate profiles into selection processes. Additionally, job profiles should be integrated into the selection process. Using these profiles can help in all of the selection methods previously described. This is critically important, because not all people are right for all roles—despite an investment in training. In some cases, the time and resources needed to get an individual to more closely match a job profile may be unrealistic. Furthermore, not all attributes that are uncovered in the competency studies and job profiling will be trainable—some you will have to hire for.

Align compensation and incentive systems with the competencies and profiles. Another support system that has to be closely integrated into the competency and job profile work is the compensation and incentive system. Too frequently, organizations reward people for behaviors that are contrary to their roles and to the relationships they are trying to build with clients. Therefore, compensation systems must reflect competencies listed for each profile as well as the progression in difficulty from one job profile to another (e.g., from account manager to senior account manager).

Establish regular checkpoints. One of the biggest takeaways from this study is that nothing is ever (or should ever be) set in stone when it comes to the sales organization. As it becomes increasingly difficult to create and maintain customer relationships, particularly those that are based on becoming a trusted business advisor, competencies will need to be revisited. Therefore, the systems and processes for selecting and developing the sales force will need to be revisited on a regular basis. The need for ongoing change and flexibility should be embedded in them.

7

REDEFINING SALES MANAGEMENT

"Five years ago, there wasn't much of a difference in skill sets [between salespeople and sales managers]. Sales leaders were the best salespeople. Now sales leaders need a good base of experience in order to understand sales as well as other parts of the organization. They need leadership skills. They need marketing skills. They need vision."

—Sales Director

Today's sales managers remain principally responsible for the development of salespeople, territories, and business for the organization. As such, sales managers bear a tremendous amount of accountability for their sales organization's overall success. As we think through the other strategies detailed in this text, it is clear that a high-performing sales management team is imperative for achieving success— whether in supporting customer relationship management (CRM) systems, developing a sales force, managing channels, deploying sales resources, or building a culture. Ironically, though, in spite of being one of the most highly valued positions within the sales structure, organizations continue to overlook this critical role. Many, if not most, sales managers are promoted to their role on the basis of their superior selling skills. Once placed, they often receive little training or support to build their leadership abilities. As a result, the role of sales manager is executed with extreme inconsistency across the sales organization.

In most sales organizations, the sales manager is structurally in the middle of the senior leaders and the frontline sales representatives. By virtue of the arrangement, this makes the sales manager the critical, if not only, bridge connecting senior management with the frontline sales representatives; in other words, they're the direct link to the marketplace. Of equal importance, sales managers also connect that same lifeline to the sales organization's owners and senior leadership. The job of the modern sales manager is as multifaceted as it is critical. It is the sales manager who

- must regularly communicate downward and upward;
- has the responsibility to turn corporate strategy and objectives into tangible field results;
- must continuously balance marketplace realities and shift with their organization's own strategy and goals;
- has to always be attuned to the larger picture and still manage the smaller details daily;
- must balance the organization's larger market strategy against individual account objectives;
- has to maintain focus on overall team or group performance, not just on individual accomplishments; and
- must respond to the call to close sales, yet develop the capabilities of the sales team to seal deals independently.

Our research found that progressive sales organizations are attempting to redefine the sales manager position and to that end are implementing initiatives to improve the management and leadership skills of those occupying this pivotal role. Against the realities of business in the early 21st century, all sales organizations should similarly be reevaluating the skills required of those occupying the sales manager seat.

Through personal interviews, the analysis of more than 2,000 critical incidents of actual sales behaviors, and a review of contemporary literature, we have discovered that sales organizations may find success by promoting a role that more evenly balances the competencies associated with the three core skill sets of strategic thinking, coaching, and communication.

CONTEMPORARY SALES MANAGER CHALLENGES

There is rarely a time when being a sales manager is easy and today is no exception. Throughout our research, sales professionals reported a number of hurdles facing their sales organizations. Some of the challenges were more external in nature, such as changes in the competitive landscape and newly emerging customer behaviors, while others were internally driven, such as reduced staffing and budgets. We examined these challenges on an organizational level in Chapter 1. Here, we look at them from a more functional perspective, illustrating how they can impact the daily responsibilities of those in a management role. Some of these challenges include:

- *More and increasingly acute competition.* Whether due to organic economic forces or the result of artificially manipulated efforts, such as deregulation, new competitors are regularly appearing on the landscape. Sales managers must have a strong pulse on competitive developments not only to personally keep current on the marketplace, but also to educate team members on competitive differentiators and revise strategies and tactics to market accordingly.
- *Increased customer and prospect demands on delivery, quality, and price.* As time passes, customer expectations rise. Many managers told us they spend a great deal of their time trying to figure out more efficient ways to meet these increased expectations and often with less resources. They focus on addressing these concerns with customers, compellingly justifying a client's or prospect's investment in

them, as well as educating their teams on how to overcome objections and sell value.

- *Changes in customer behavior.* Nearly every organization we encountered reported some change in customer behavior. Each of these developments has direct implications on the ability of salespeople to maintain and mature personal relationships, traditionally a successful sales technique. For sales managers, the impact is significant as they must become creative in developing solutions to overcoming these barriers to relationship building. Further, they need to have the skills to teach and coach their sales teams to be equally innovative in the creation of alternative approaches and techniques.

- *Greater urgency on the part of stakeholders to exceed revenue and profit goals.* Alongside the tentative economic conditions of the early 21st century, owners and principal stakeholders placed considerable value on those who acquired profitable business. This shift now requires sales managers to fully understand the financial impact each deal will have on their own organization's bottom line. Likewise, it forces the sales manager to educate his or her field associates on identifying business opportunities that will yield acceptable returns for the enterprise.

- *Sales organization reductions.* In an effort to reduce the cost of sales and achieve maximum profit, sales organizations across the globe have likewise taken similar steps, such as reducing or completely removing support and administrative positions, consolidating territories, slashing field positions, decreasing sales bonuses and incentives, and cutting back on recognition programs. Each of these actions requires a sales manager who can effectively make allocation decisions, including staffing, for maximum return, while simultaneously keeping sales force morale up.

- *Managing more channels to market.* Sales managers, unlike their predecessors of generations past, may be responsible for managing a mixture of avenues to market, each with its own unique nuances and each presenting distinct challenges unto themselves. The presence of multiple channels also increases the potential for conflict, reinforcing the need for sales managers to be both proficient at tailoring strategies for unique channel points and to possess strong conflict resolution skills.

- *Improvements in sales force technology.* Technological advancement, like a double-edged sword, presents the sales organization with opportunities and challenges. For the sales manager, sales force automation (SFA) systems can provide a host of valuable and insightful information for tracking team performance, managing resources, and quickly identifying gaps. For optimal success to be achieved, however, the sales manager must have field representatives and others keeping critical information up-to-date and accurate. Moreover, they must facilitate an environment that secures the complete buy-in for these tools and their maintenance from field associates. Without frontline acceptance, the outputs of these tools are meaningless.

THE SKILLS REQUIRED FOR SUCCESSFUL SALES MANAGEMENT

We believe successful sales managers must posses a carefully balanced blend of technical and soft skills. While a strong foundation of technical skills—for example, forecasting, competitive analysis, and quota setting—is required of all sales managers, sales leaders achieve results through people, not machines or software alone, and hence the importance of the people skills required of this critical role.

Again, in addition to our personal interviews with sales organizations around the world, we also conducted a critical incident study with 500 sales professionals across 10 countries. All told, we found specific competencies that define success in sales management. In turn, we grouped these competencies into three specific roles—Stategist, Coach, and Communicator. Depending on the situation at hand, some roles may play a more important part than others; however, experience in all three roles is required for success.

In the final analysis, the competencies for successful sales management identified in our research are significantly different from those found in other independent studies for front-line sales professionals. For instance, sales managers must make decisions that advance their organization's market strategy whereas individual salespeople make decisions aligned with particular account strategies. Further, just as it is important for sales managers to maintain a keen focus on team performance, salespeople on the other hand are solely responsible for their own performance. Consider also, sales managers have a responsibility to educate their salespeople to close a deal versus executing the final deal each time themselves.

Overall, our findings for successful sales management, when compared to those for successful salespeople, support the commonly understood fact that the best salespeople don't always make the best sales managers. Next, we examine in-depth the roles of Strategist, Coach, and Communicator.

The Strategist

The Strategist role is generally viewed as the toughest for a sales manager. This role requires an individual who can concurrently see the "bigger picture" and keep a sharp eye on the smaller details. A balanced thinker—who is mindful of strategic objectives while managing actual performance—contributes heavily to establishing direction and building team confidence. The Strategist must be skilled at communicating the vision, developing a market strategy, managing resources, and maintaining a current knowledge base.

The role of the Strategist is to:

- Communicate a vision.
- Develop a market strategy.
- Manage resources.
- Maintain a current knowledge base.

Communicating the vision. This ability is essential for both efficiency and effectiveness. In *Leadership Is an Art,* Max DePree declares that "the first responsibility of a leader is to define reality." It's true, sales managers who can successfully bring their sales teams across the finish line are often those who can define a vision for it.

Within the strategic role, the sales manager often will act as a final decision maker; tasked with making decisions that advance organizational objectives. For example, they must determine how and where to allocate resources, which business opportunities to pursue and likewise which to abandon, and which sales terms to accept and which to decline. Simultaneously, they support and enforce company policies and develop and communicate the organization's mission and vision.

Sometimes that vision may be as simple as a clear "stretch goal"—that is, an objective everyone can rally around. One sales manager shared with us that she was able to beat her quota using such a unifying objective. She said, "I established a stretch goal for us and at every monthly meeting the very first topic was the stretch goal. I made it clear how each individual would be impacted if we reached the goal. I think the team internalized the stretch goal and realized we could make steady progress. We didn't hit the stretch goal but we clearly overachieved our target goal."

So why is it so important to be constantly creating, communicating, and executing the vision? As stated many times throughout this book, all sales organizations are in a constant state of flux. Today this involves redefining customer segments, reassigning territories, and revisiting sales processes; all the more reason why steady communication of the common objective is so crucial to keeping the team focused. Additionally, it also supports the sales team's ability to deliver a consistent message to market.

Developing a market strategy. This next competency involves analyzing the marketplace—for example, determining its size and potential, assessing the competition, and uncovering trends. This competency also includes developing business development plans, such as advertisements, direct mail campaigns, and marketing events.

Not too long ago, sales managers had discretionary budgets for local marketing initiatives. In today's world of tightened budgets this practice is becoming more infrequent. Perhaps more than ever before, local territories are completely dependant on centralized corporate marketing initiatives that may be based in another state—or even in another continent. While this may appear ironic, often the sales organization has not been able to show a hard return on these initiatives and in current business conditions cannot simply justify this type of investment on the basis of "we've always done it that way."

The lesson here: Sales managers must align themselves closer with the marketing function instead of working around it. As one sales manager put it, "I could not tolerate having a discussion with marketing people—they didn't understand the business, they dealt with fluff, they thought they knew everything. But I also realized that we needed help in our local market. Now, I work with them at presenting to local business groups—they help craft our proposals, and they even help sales reps with their presentations."

Managing resources. Managing resources effectively, another critical activity by virtue of the nature of business itself, may be the most time-consuming competency as it involves the following:

- Securing resources, including people, money, and supplies
- Managing staff or headcount based on performance data and budgetary controls
- Managing multiple distribution channels to maximize market penetration
- Selecting and recruiting the right talent

Possibly most challenging of all is taking responsibility for the team's contribution to the organization's bottom line. Sales managers are accountable for managing budgets and expenditures, as well as ensuring that sales contracts are constructed to meet organizational goals, mine client opportunities, and ensure organizational parameters are being met.

Talent management can be a full-time responsibility in its own right. A sales manager's most precious resource is the individuals who comprise the sales team. Mismanaging voluntary or involuntary attrition can have devastating consequences for the team's overall success. Sales managers must be skilled at retaining top talent during good and bad times and likewise capable of making balanced staffing decisions as downsizing initiatives require. Organizations that fail to have clearly defined career paths and development plans can thwart a sales manager's success.

While each channel to market helps an organization extend its presence, it also can serve as a source of many headaches for sales managers. As the number of distribution channels increases, especially those with self-serve options, such as the Internet and the telephone, so too can the propensity for more discord with other channels, such as direct sales forces and account teams, among others. To effectively manage conflicts, the organization needs to make channel distinctions crystal clear and up front.

Earlier in the chapter we noted that sales managers are often in the middle. Sales force compensation is one of those issues where being in the center may consume a lot of time because sales managers are frequently called upon to interpret ever-changing commission structures. Cichelli (2003) reports that "95 percent of all companies expect to change their sales compensation plans for 2004." While there is no magic formula for creating the perfect plan, you can minimize stress by developing a plan that is aligned with the organization's strategy, defines desired salesperson behaviors and results, and determines what can actually be measured and thus rewarded before cascading the plan down the organization.

Maintaining a current knowledge base. This final competency rounds out the Strategist requirements. It involves keeping product, market, and competitive knowledge current. When a salesperson is promoted to a management position, they often become consumed by administrative functions and hence rest on the laurels of previously acquired market, product, and competitive information. Unfortunately, such information becomes outdated quickly.

In the sports world, an "agent" gets the business; however, it's the "team manager" who knows the sport, the individual athletes, and the overall game plan. We find that given the time and delivery pressures placed on sales managers, they tend to migrate toward the agent model. They know the logistics of accessing resources and product training, but they don't fully know the products, the marketplace, or the current selling environment. Most unfortunately, they sometimes don't really know their own team members' specific strengths and weaknesses.

One sales manager we spoke with had a clever way of keeping his competitive information up-to-date. He would hold monthly role-play sessions with his sales team and have them pretend to sell for and against the competition. Not only did this help their selling skills but it also helped him keep in touch with team member talents and what was happening competitively in the marketplace. It cannot be overemphasized that listening to salespeople in the field is one of the best ways to keep market knowledge current.

Potential Pitfalls in the Strategist Role

A common profile is of a sales manager who is almost exclusively a Strategist. This person excels at planning and is often referred to as a visionary. While such sales managers possess a clear understanding of their market and their product's current and future place in it, they sometimes find themselves disappointed in their team's inability to make this vision a reality. In fact, more often than not, the sales team doesn't even understand what the vision is and is prone to view this manager as "sitting in an ivory tower"—disconnected from the salesperson's reality and hard to approach.

The Coach

The Coach role is about cultivating high-performance behaviors and processes within the sales force—from advice on specific situations to the development of long-term career plans. The traditional image of a sales manager often conjures the likeness of a coach, and sales managers, just like coaches, yield great influence with their teams—both positive and negative—through their attitude and actions.

While this role is typically deemed the most important by sales professionals, it is often neglected, especially in times when sales are slow, budgets are limited, and increasing administrative responsibilities consume the day's agenda. This is a real concern. According to a 2002 *Sales & Marketing Management*/Equation Research (2002) survey, over a third of the sales executives reported that their sales managers spent less than five hours per week coaching their field associates. (See Figure 7.1.)

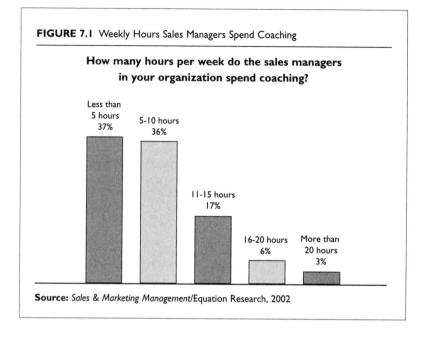

FIGURE 7.1 Weekly Hours Sales Managers Spend Coaching

How many hours per week do the sales managers in your organization spend coaching?

Source: *Sales & Marketing Management/Equation Research*, 2002

Responsibilities of a Coach include building cohesive teams, assisting with sales activities, developing professional skills, and motivating individuals. These activities are discussed below in more detail.

The role of the coach is to:

- Build cohesive teams.
- Assist with sales activities.
- Develop professional skills and careers.
- Motivate individuals.

Building a cohesive team. To build a cohesive team requires the sales manager to bring diverse personalities together, in some collaborative and cooperative way, to deliver hard results. Whether a team is built from scratch or inherited, chances are high it will be comprised of individuals with a range of talents, experiences, tenure, and geographic posts. This is further complicated by the continuous restructuring that occurs in sales organizations today.

Just like any other workplace team, a sales team too must be stronger than the sum of its parts. This may be demonstrated through the team's ability to rally around critical projects and share information among its members. The sales manager needs to create an environment with equitable treatment, respect, and robust team spirit conducive to constructive conflict resolution and decision making.

Effective sales managers may achieve tangible results by recruiting the best, setting performance standards through instruction and constructive feedback, and by recognizing and capitalizing on those with the greatest potential for success.

Assisting with sales activities. This is one of the trickiest skills to master. While it's critical to coaching and helps a manager gain respect from the sales team, there is always the danger that the manager will become too involved in the sales process, in effect, becoming a salesperson again. Usually, however, time-constrained managers will err on the side of too little involvement. In fact, a recent *Sales & Marketing Management/*Equation Research survey (2002) of 455 sales managers found that nearly 42 percent had not been on a sales call in the past month. (See Figure 7.2.)

When the ride along does occur, the real challenge for sales managers is to maintain their focus on coaching—assisting in the actual call and resisting the temptation to completely take over and become a salesperson again. They simply don't have the time to take on that role and, moreover, it contradicts their overall objective: to enhance their salesperson's credibility in the eyes of customers and prospects and coach them for better individual performance.

Successful sales managers support activities throughout the sales cycle by using their network of contacts to identify prospects; leveraging their understanding of the bigger picture; draw-

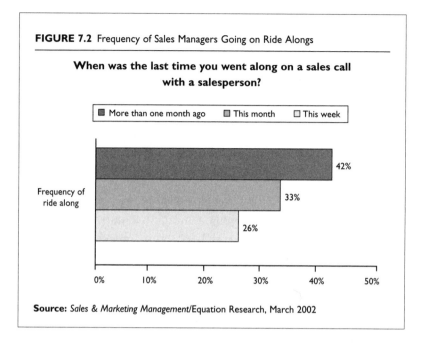

FIGURE 7.2 Frequency of Sales Managers Going on Ride Alongs

When was the last time you went along on a sales call with a salesperson?

Legend: ■ More than one month ago ▨ This month □ This week

Frequency of ride along:
- More than one month ago: 42%
- This month: 33%
- This week: 26%

Source: *Sales & Marketing Management*/Equation Research, March 2002

ing on their depth of experience to strategize account plans; and, ultimately, helping to close business.

Effective sales managers also will skillfully intervene in contentious customer interactions, targeting conflict resolution in a way that satisfies the customer and preserves the salesperson's account relationship.

At the end of the day, team members need to trust their sales manager to participate at the appropriate level and help develop their capabilities. One sales manager shared, "Every salesperson knows that clients need to trust them. If a salesperson cannot build trust, they will not succeed. I feel the same way with my relationship with my salespeople: If they can't trust me, I will not succeed."

Developing professional skills and careers. Assisting salespeople in developing their professional skills and careers is probably the best investment managers can make with their time.

Effective sales managers recognize that teams are comprised of individuals. To maximize efforts, the performance of all members—not just the lesser performers—must be improved. This can be done through behavioral observation, skills assessment, and targeted coaching and training, such as skill- and knowledge-based instruction. The sales manager's goal is to build future capabilities.

This is similar to the old story about the value of teaching a man to fish, as he will be better equipped to survive long term than by merely giving him the fish so he can make it through one meal. As we engage with sales organizations around the world, we find that many are still trying to implement a consistent consultative selling approach. We see that one of their biggest hurdles is ensuring that taught skills are reinforced and modeled by sales managers. A great illustration of this was shared by a top-tier salesperson who said, "The most successful and motivating thing I have experienced is the *genuine* desire and support of a sales manager to help a rep be the best sales professional he or she can be. I had a sales manager that once told me, 'Whether you stay or leave this company, I can't control that, but I do want you to be the best salesperson you can regardless.'"

The sales organization may yield better results from fewer opportunities when it provides support training and guidance to field associates and has sales managers who observe sales calls, model skills, mentor, and regularly review performance. The presence and use of formal performance and development tools (e.g., job profiles, competency assessments, coaching evaluations checklists, as well as applications and reinforcement job aids) also helps.

Motivating individuals. This is the final key to being a good Coach. In addition to developing sales professionals, effective sales managers motivate performance in ways that extend far beyond incentive programs and quota plans. They use motivational methods, such as verbal recognition, performance management, and communication, to encourage the team and evoke enthusiasm. However, each person is different and is motivated by different factors. What appeals to a recent college graduate may not work with experienced sales professionals. Sales managers need to work a bit differently with each person; it's much less about the manager's style and more about the salesperson's style.

It is this kind of coaching behavior that is most easily recalled by sales superstars and most often attributed to good

Walking the Talk at Office Depot

To combat increasing competitive threats, Office Depot's Business Services Group (BSG) decided to revamp the selling skills of their account executives through a comprehensive training and development curriculum. However, they didn't start training the sales teams right away. They knew that success had to start not with the field, but first with the sales managers. If the sales managers weren't properly skilled and weren't modeling and reinforcing the training back on the job, the organization would never succeed at achieving any behavior change.

Therefore, before any training was rolled out to the field, all sales managers (and for that matter, directors and VPs too) went through selling skills courses and coaching programs. The goal was to make sure that managers not only could model the selling skills expected of their teams but that they would also be able to coach to those behaviors.

In addition to training, managers also were supplied with a variety of tools that could be used back on the job. They received coaching forms that helped them document coaching observations, prepare for coaching conversations, and give feedback in writing. They also were provided with toolkits that helped them facilitate brief selling skills practices with their salespeople. Sales managers then used these tools to integrate development activity into regular sales meetings.

managers. But motivating individuals is hard to do, especially if the sales manager is not being motivated by his or her own superiors. We spoke with a salesperson who recalled the words of a previous sales manager, spoken some ten years earlier yet still true today, who said, "Great years are made up of great quarters. Great quarters are made up of great months. Great months are made up of great weeks. Great weeks are made up of great days. Great days are made up of great hours. Great hours are made up of great moments. Is what you're doing right now creating or preparing you for a great moment?"

Potential Pitfalls in the Coach Role

Sales managers who devote their time to coaching but do not fulfill the other roles can be successful, but they may not unleash the full potential of their staff. They are generally well liked, consistently model the selling skills needed by their employees, and are diligent about developing individuals and teams through training.

While such sales managers may be able to manage a mature market, they are likely to experience difficulties expanding their region beyond organic growth and are frequently out of touch with corporate objectives.

The Communicator

The last role is that of the Communicator, which may be considered the foundation for the Coach and Strategist roles. Two of the most important roles a sales manager performs are 1) acting as a liaison between top management and the sales staff, and 2) creating a culture of information sharing.

This role describes the characteristics that ensure the flow of information throughout the sales organization is timely and accurate. A good communicator will not accept missed opportunities due to misunderstandings and the lack of infrastructure and technology. The Communicator role includes, of course, being able to communicate across the organization, but more specifically, keeping the field informed; soliciting and valuing feedback; and facilitating information sharing both up and down the organization.

The role of the Communicator is to:

- Communicate across the organization.
- Keep the field informed.
- Solicit and value feedback.
- Facilitate information sharing.

Communicating information across the organization. Communicating information helps ensure that field and market information can be shared across the entire organization—beyond just the sales department. One of the biggest time demands for today's sales managers is to act as the liaison between the field and headquarters and between the sales organization and other parts of the enterprise. Effective sales managers are able to work closely with all parts of the organization to ensure team success. They are diligent about providing progress report details and communicating the factors—positive and negative—that impact the team's ability to meet and exceed expectations.

In today's business climate, accurate forecasting, for example, is more critical than ever as this information is receiving much higher visibility. Furthermore, not hitting predictions has greater ramifications today than, say, five years ago. Because forecasts, even for individual accounts, are moving much further up in the organization ranks, sales managers must spend considerable efforts scrubbing these reports—at the expense of consuming limited and valuable time.

In addition, sales managers are often responsible for documenting all sales activities to show superiors what their team is doing, for justifying resource allocations, and for making the organization's external activities visible to others—still more tasks that take considerable time to complete. According to a *Sales & Marketing Management*/Equation Research (2002) survey, 47 percent of sales managers reported that they spend more time on paperwork today than they did two years ago. This same survey found that for the most part, sales managers are feeling the pressures of administrative functions. Consider Figure 7.3.

Successful sales managers also have the responsibility to pave the way for interdepartmental cooperation, acting as advocates for the field. One sales manager offered, "I make sure I join any internal committee or task force that is looking for new product ideas. It not only allows me to influence future products, but I make new contacts and learn about new strategies or campaigns before they happen."

Without question, today's sales managers are spending too much time on communication via reporting. The challenge for successful sales management is not the completion of the tasks or the accounts themselves, but rather, the amount of time these managers are investing to perform this function. In the end, it is ultimately limiting their involvement with more crucial field responsibilities, such as coaching salespeople and visiting with customers. To overcome the challenge, sales managers must

FIGURE 7.3 Managerial Administrative Duties

Statement	Percent Agree
The time I spend on administrative duties cuts into the time I would be spending with customers.	73%
In general, sales managers these days are overburdened with administrative duties and red tape.	72
Administrative duties cut into time I would be spending out in the field with salespeople.	67
The shaky economy has caused me to devote more of my time to administrative duties.	49

Source: *Sales & Marketing Management*/Equation Research, December 2002

employ a time management technique, including effective delegating, that will allow them to accomplish these tasks as efficiently as possible.

From an organizational perspective, and to further refine what information is truly needed, the sales manager should assess the amount and quality of data collected and satisfactorily answer four key questions:

1. Is there consistency in what we are measuring? For example, are all parties utilizing the same forecasting methodology?
2. Are there systems currently available that could make data retrieval and reporting less time-intensive?
3. What are end users doing with the data that is reported?
4. How often do end users really need this information?

Keeping the field informed is the flip side of the coin. Managers as information conduits ensure that the field is receiving the information they need to do their jobs in a way that supports the strategy. Nothing is more counterproductive than organizations acting at cross-purposes. For example, the marketing department has invested in a campaign to push a particular product, while the sales team is sending out direct mail pieces promoting another product all together. Successful sales managers prevent this situation from happening by ensuring that the staff is communicated to and understands the corporate market and product strategies.

Keeping the field informed is a competency about sustaining open lines of communication with the sales team and continuously communicating organizational changes and corporate strategies. Without this open and continuous communication, high levels of employee dissatisfaction can result, leading to reduced productivity and high turnover. One organization we spoke with had recently laid off thousands. They felt the key to keeping retained staff motivated was continuous and open communication. Their president held periodic telecasts where he outlined the state of the business and short- and long-term plans to make sure employees felt like they were in the loop.

Many times it's not just the message that gets delivered to salespeople, but it's also the manner it's delivered. The best managers, sales and nonsales, act as "filters" not "amplifiers." So many times sales managers receive the brunt of senior management's frustrations and then carry the same message, but louder, back to their salespeople. Instead, managers need to filter that message into something that is useful to the sales team and actionable. Independent of communication style, the key is to make sure the sharing of information occurs because silence or complete avoidance is a problem that can ratchet up employee dissatisfaction and attrition.

Soliciting and valuing feedback. This step helps complete the communication loop. Effective sales managers create an environment where the sales team perceives that input and feedback is valued. Communication should not be a one-way street from the manager to the team. Sales representatives know better than anyone what their customers are saying and what they want. In fact, they are usually closer to the customer than any other person in the organization.

Sales managers should regularly encourage salespeople to express opinions and participate in policy development. They should also incorporate their team's input when making decisions. The presence of remote field associates makes it all the more important that sales managers make their team members feel valued and included in decisions that impact their operations. Sales representatives who feel isolated can have disastrous consequences on team performance.

A good practice for any manager to follow, sales-related or not, is to ask for opinions and suggestions on how to handle different situations. This can be a valuable tactic for getting both a fresh perspective on an issue and field buy-in to a new policy

A *Commitment to Coaching at BellSouth*

BellSouth Corporation, based in Atlanta, Georgia, is a Fortune 100 communication services company. The company and its partners serve more than 45 million local, long distance, Internet, and wireless customers in the United States and 13 other countries.

The company's small business services division, which targets businesses spending $3,000 or less per month on telecommunication services, offers local, long distance, wireless, high-speed Internet access, and multisite fiber connections to small businesses across a nine-state region in the Southeastern United States.

In response to a number of marketplace developments, the small business services division restructured its sales organization. Today the division is segmented into an inbound customer retention sales group and an outbound/premise channel responsible for developing new business and reacquiring lost customers.

As part of the strategy to improve sales effectiveness, the company instituted a series of hard (sales process standards) and soft (selling training and reinforcement) tools. Other processes involving metrics, scorecards, daily measures of call volume, and proposals, along with new performance management standards, were also implemented.

These strategies were further promoted and supported through the creation of the complex applications specialists (CAS) team and sales effectiveness coaches (SEC). The CAS team supports the outbound reacquisition group and reactively supports inbound sales relationship and retention managers. They also assist with customers that have complex telecommunication needs by offering wider technological solutions and with proposals involving more sophisticated technologies requiring the services of other BellSouth operating divisions.

The SEC has evolved into "a regional SWAT team" staffed with one coach per center. The coaches deliver workshops, support sales development through active coaching, and work with account representatives "to act as a change agent."

or initiative. But be careful to not ask salespeople for feedback if you are not going to use it or be able to address it. Doing nothing has a more negative effect than not asking for it at all.

Facilitating information sharing. Facilitating information sharing across the team leads to a more collaborative environment and helps the organization learn from its experiences. Successful sales managers not only communicate effectively with their teams and upper management, they also actively promote open and honest communication among and between sales teams. Because sales professionals spend so much time in the field, often working remotely too, they sometimes require formal practices and structures to promote both professional and personal communication with their colleagues.

Managers can actively encourage the sharing of information, problems, or concerns among the sales team by providing opportunities to network, holding cross-team meetings, requiring collaboration for certain activities, and creating mentoring programs.

Making information sharing a standard operating procedure is largely the responsibility of the sales manager, and it can be a difficult one at best. This involves not simply selecting and implementing a mechanism for doing it but also creating the culture in which it is supported. There are two potential obstacles to establishing such an arrangement. First, SFA and CRM systems traditionally have been used for managerial purposes rather than to facilitate information sharing among salespeople. To that end, it is not uncommon to encounter salespeople who will question the value of complying with data entry requests only to "get beaten up by my manager with the data I enter." Our research has found, at least anecdotally, the fears of "big brother" are alive and well in many sales organizations.

Another concern in creating an information-sharing culture is more technical as backfilling Intranet portals with large amounts of information can become problematic and hard to navigate in the absence of an overall knowledge management strategy.

No one can deny technology's potential to support the sales process, as we know many of the key activities and measurements we've discussed could be enabled through a technical solution. Unfortunately, though, most technological tools continue to be primarily used for management and reporting purposes at high levels and for little else.

Potential Pitfalls in the Communicator Role

A manager totally devoted to fulfilling the Communicator role is fully focused on collecting and sharing information. This person is diligent about completing progress reports and consistently uses contact reporting and tracking systems.

Unfortunately, this manager is viewed as an administrator and is often unable to move their territory beyond status quo. According to one research participant, this kind of person "can be great with details but misses the big picture."

THE IMPACT OF MANAGEMENT STYLE

In addition to the three roles, we also discovered that salespeople attribute a certain style to managers they perceive as being more successful. Based on the responses of those interviewed, an "enabling" management style facilitates the sales manager's ability to execute the three roles, thereby facilitating salesperson peak performance.

While the indicators that point to an enabling management style cannot be specifically linked to success, respondents perceive their importance in fulfilling the three key roles. Although the sales professionals we interviewed often characterized sales managers on a continuum between polar extremes, we noted that these descriptions were usually based on the relative success of the manager.

Those identified as having an enabling manager style were more successful meeting quotas, while those with an inhibiting style were reported to have turnover and revenue problems. Even though this style of management is not a requirement, it does make things much easier and contributes to the creation of more loyal staff committed to exceeding organizational goals. The key attributes of the Enabler are:

- Consistently considers different perspectives.
- Listens to the concerns of individuals with compassion and patience.
- Keeps promises and leads by example.
- Exhibits enthusiasm, confidence, commitment, and honesty.

BEST PRACTICES AND LESSONS LEARNED

While sales managers may feel trapped in the middle of the high-performing sales organization, they are not alone. Other parts of the organization, such as training and development, marketing, and senior executives, will have great influence over whether the sales manager will be able to succeed in each of these roles.

It is important to remember that not all competencies, or even a high level of proficiency in each, are required for all situations. In fact, there are many instances when a sales manager only needs to draw on one or two of the roles. Ultimately, however, all three roles are required to optimize the performance of the sales team. Even a team of "superstars" needs a manager who can successfully navigate all three. Our research found that while sales managers typically excel in one of these roles and demonstrate strengths and weaknesses in others, very few managers have mastered all three.

Therefore, an integrated curriculum should be created that helps sales managers bridge from selling skills into these competencies. One organization, well on its way in such development work, began by evaluating their managers using a competency assessment. As a direct result, they initiated a 30 percent turnover in their management team. They simply felt like they had too many of the wrong people in the wrong positions. Sometimes this kind of aggressive restructuring can be beneficial. Other times, it will distract and derail an organization. The key is to have a clear set of standards established such that you can make an accurate assessment of sales manager talent.

8

CREATING A CULTURE FOR WINNING SALES

"Everything we do, including recruiting, training, and recognition, reinforces our culture. In the end we know that we win sales by having stable, high-flying, high-charged sales reps who are caught up in what they do."

—Sales Manager

Successful sales strategies depend on the ability of the sales organization to create a culture that supports and reinforces the decisions, activities, goals, and behaviors required to execute the strategy. Moreover, the culture must maintain strategy momentum, transform the vision of the strategy into action, and ensure that everyone is aligned and committed to success.

Although culture is a rather abstract notion, particularly for salespeople who are focused on tactics and bottom-line results, the symbols, expectations, and behaviors that define and reinforce a culture are very real and tangible. This chapter focuses on the importance of a sales culture in executing strategies, and the critical need for thinking about developing the best sales culture as a strategy unto itself. The chapter is not about recommending the best culture to adopt but it's more about the important components or characteristics that a culture must possess to successfully implement strategies that win sales.

Each of the strategies discussed in this book, such as consultative selling, sales and customer segmentation, and customer resource management (CRM) system implementation, require cultural alignment and support. For example, a consultative selling strategy requires a customer-focused culture, representing a shift, for many organizations, from focusing on selling products to selling solutions that increase customer productivity and value. Similarly, successful CRM strategies require a sales culture that facilitates and supports the adoption of CRM applications by making it a part of everyone's daily business activities.

A well-defined culture is particularly important for salespeople because they are physically separated from the rest of the organization and therefore require some type of formal structure to guide their behavior in the absence of everyday reinforcement from managers and colleagues. Because salespeople often wear several hats in addition to selling, such as customer service, marketing, and administrative, norms and values are required to help clarify role ambiguities. Moreover, culture defines immediate rewards that are important when tangible sales results take time to materialize. In addition, the sales force presents an important face of the company to customers and the outside world. As such, salespeople must accurately communicate and model the culture in the marketplace so that the company's reputation and image are properly conveyed. If the culture is not well defined, customers may get mixed signals about what type of company their salesperson represents.

While creating a sales culture is important for guiding behavior and establishing norms and standards for the organization, a culture is only effective when it is aligned with the company's objectives, strategies, industry, and business environment, which will be discussed in more detail later in this chapter. First, we'll define culture and focus on why it's important for winning sales.

ORGANIZATIONAL AND
SALES FORCE CULTURE

The notion of culture often is considered a rather abstract concept; something that's difficult to observe and explain in a tangible way, but nonetheless very real. Underlying all organizations are unique values and beliefs that guide how members of that company make decisions and perform their work on a daily basis. According to Schein (1984), corporate culture can be defined as a "system of behaviors, rituals, and shared meaning held by employees that distinguish a group or organization." The norms and values of a company's culture are rooted in its organizational history, typically defined by founders or leaders of the organization, and communicated through formal and informal mechanisms.

Most discussions about culture begin with the norms, values, and beliefs that shape the behavior of employees and guide decision making. While a norm describes how an individual should behave when confronting a choice, values guide how an individual should aspire to behave. Although underlying components of a culture generally remain constant, norms, values, and work styles, or the actual activities and behaviors of employees, often evolve over time. The norms and values that work well and lead to successful outcomes are reinforced, while those cultural characteristics that lose their purpose or relevancy are abandoned. This evolution, along with changes in leadership, can result in shifts in corporate culture.

In a more tangible way, norms and values are manifested through stated "guiding principles" that are modeled consistently by management and through managerial decisions. These principles define behavior around operations, roles, responsibilities, employee and customer interactions, corporate social responsibility, and daily work activities. The stronger a culture is, the more likely employees are to live by these principles and

Sales Culture Is Key to Success at Yellow Book USA

"The user first, advertiser second, and Yellow Book third"—the mantra that can be recited by any Yellow Book salesperson—reflects the cultural values and norms guiding every decision and behavior throughout the company. This simple motto means that salespeople must first do what is in the best interest of the users of their yellow pages—those consumers who refer to the yellow pages when searching for a business listing. Yellow Book wants their directories to be the consumers' first choice. The next priority is given to the company's customers: the advertisers. According to the culture, no matter how small, each and every advertiser is important to Yellow Book. As one company official said, "Every account counts for Yellow Book. We build the business because we care more than the competitor about our accounts, and we take no account for granted—no matter how small." Finally, after taking care of the customer and the advertiser, salespeople must do what's best for the company.

Yellow Book prides itself on its sales culture and strengthens that culture by making the sales force a priority. Yellow Book has built a career ladder that clearly demonstrates where and how salespeople can grow, and they recruit those who have the desire, work ethic, and passion to be the best at what they do. The company views the sales force as its greatest asset, aiming to make Yellow Book the "last company you'll ever work for," meaning that "this is a company where an employee's personal and career goals can be met as they grow." If Yellow Book is passionate about one thing, it is people development, and their intense focus on training proves this point. Salespeople go through ongoing training and even sales managers participate in regular manager conferences designed to instill in them Yellow Book's core values.

In the end, the company feels that it is successful and is confident that it will beat the competition by maintaining a culture of "stable, high-flying, high-charged sales reps who are caught up in what they do."

the more willing they are to perform the tasks to accomplish the company's mission.

As with corporate culture, sales culture provides salespeople with the ground rules for being successful members of the organization, provides a central theme around which salespeople's behavior may be focused, and affects sales force productivity through its influence on how sales organizations socialize new salespeople and respond to market challenges. A sales culture instills discipline by establishing daily sales processes and activities, and a well-managed sales force culture improves communication, morale, and motivation. It also provides salespeople direction in terms of behavior that is supported by the organization and that ultimately impacts performance.

According to Ott (1989), the content and structure of a sales culture is composed of three levels. The first level is made up of visible and audible artifacts that define and perpetuate the culture. Level two requires consciously held beliefs that govern the behavior of employees, and level three involves basic assumptions and ideologies that are so ingrained in the beliefs held by the employees that they are more or less subconscious. Jackson (1994) defines the components of each level as detailed next.

Level 1. Artifacts and patterns of behavior. Examples of culture at this level include the following:

- *Symbols,* which communicate information about the beliefs and values of the organization. They are usually objects, such as plaques or trophies, that members identify with the overall culture.
- *Language,* which includes the words or phrases that are attached to a culture and have special meaning in the organization. These may be made-up words, but they are understood by everyone in the organization.

- *Myths/stories,* which describe a company's beginning, history, and desired direction with past events and employees' actions and that display the essence of the mission and values. One company always tells a story about a sales representative that called the CEO of a prospective customer every day for two months. He finally got a call back and it became the biggest account landed in years. This story has been passed from team to team for years.
- *Heroes,* who personify the values of the organization and provide role models for salespeople to follow. One company named a sales award after a successful and popular salesperson who had been with the company for many years and recently passed away.
- *Rituals,* which are activities of the organization that include evaluation procedures, meetings, work scheduling, and indoctrination practices. One telecommunications company surveyed requires their salespeople to attend a two-week training class at the end of their first year. This training event has become a right of passage for salespeople as they move from rookie to the next stage in the sales organization.
- *Celebrations,* which acknowledge the contributions of successful members and display the culture both internally and externally. Celebrations include annual quota trips, national sales meetings, and other events that have become "traditions."

Level 2. Values and beliefs. At this level in the culture, the following are well defined:

- *Values,* which represent what an organization stands for, what its members believe in, and what its members must do. Values for several of the organizations we spoke with included such things as "integrity," "fairness," and "superior work ethic," among others. As one company representative described a value, "We operate with extreme morality in a marketplace that is often ripe with misleading information."

- *Beliefs,* which are ideas members perceive to be true. Such ideas that a company's products are the highest quality in the industry, that salespeople are the cream of the crop, or that managers are always there to support their salespeople are some of the "beliefs" we heard in our interviews.

Level 3. Assumptions. Basic ideologies and assumptions are found in this third level of culture, as noted by the following:

- *Fundamental perceptions,* which are implicit and consistent throughout the organization and guide how members behave and think and feel about things. Members make their own decisions about how to behave based on their assumptions of the culture.

On all levels, culture can be understood by observing the work styles and activities of employees that reflect how people act, make decisions, and interact with each other and with the outside world.

While the sales culture is reflected and guided by the greater organizational culture, sales cultures are different and often exhibit distinct behaviors from the rest of the organization because of the unique work activities of salespeople. Salespeople differ from other functions in their roles and responsibilities as well as in other areas, such as their proximity to headquarters, level of customer interactions, and compensation structures. Salespeople often work alone and are distant from headquarters, in most cases resulting in a lot less exposure to the organization's culture. The sales organization, as a whole, generally meets only a few times per year at most, while other functional areas may meet on a weekly or even daily basis.

Sales cultures also differ, and take on a different level of importance, in their values guiding performance, collaboration, and interactions with the customer. Unlike others in the organization, the daily work activities of salespeople are not readily observable by the rest of the organization, yet their outcomes are measurable and individual performance is usually communicated to the rest of the sales organization if not the entire company. While teamwork and collaboration are highly valued in most office environments, the sales force is by nature often more competitive than collaborative. Finally, sales activities are externally focused on the customer, whereas most other functions in the organization are internally focused on operations required to run the company. These differences may not mean that their culture must be distinct from the rest of the organization, but they do require unique mechanisms (symbols, language, and incentives, for example) through which the culture is reinforced.

Content of a Sales Culture

The makeup of a sales culture can be very different from organization to organization. Cultures differ in their underlying values and beliefs and the priorities placed on them within the organization. The shared languages, behaviors, and attitudes that characterize sales cultures may include a host of attributes. As we'll discuss later in this chapter, regardless of how many attributes are selected to define a culture, the content of the sales culture must align with the organization's strategies and objectives, and their business and industry environment.

While cultural constructs may be complex and there may be many characteristics that compose the content of a culture, leading sales organizations are able to boil them down to a handful of powerful yet simple concepts. The organizations we interviewed, for example, characterized sales cultures in a variety of ways: "competitive and hardworking"; "encouraged to take risks and think outside of the box"; "empowered to make customer-focused decisions"; "team-oriented and collaborative." These characteristics can be extended to individual characteristics as well. For example, one company preferred a sales culture of seasoned sales professionals, while another looked for sales reps who were "young and enthusiastic."

There are no inherently right or wrong values or norms that make up a culture—some organizations may encourage cut-throat competitiveness as part of the culture, while others value team work and collaboration—what is important is that they are the right components given the company's strategies, objectives, and business environment. The following are a few of the attributes organizations in our study used to describe their sales cultures:

- Encourages experimenting with different selling techniques.
- Is team-oriented and collaborative.
- Is adaptive and flexible.
- Maintains accountability.
- Is fair and compassionate.
- Encourages taking initiative and making decisions independently.
- Is socially and environmentally responsible.
- Promotes healthy internal competition.
- Takes risks.
- Focuses on the competition.
- Confronts conflict directly.

The content of a sales culture—the mix of norms, values, and standards that guide actions and attitudes—can be complex. However, the culture is more effective if it can be conveyed in simple yet all-encompassing words or phrases. It is important to remember that an organization must make a conscious effort to proactively create and maintain cultural content instead of just allowing one to develop and accepting passively what norms and values develop. Only then can the optimal culture be created and fostered, as well as controlled. Next we discuss why it is important to have a sales culture in terms of performance and we review how successful organizations create cultures that win sales.

Why Have a Sales Culture?

Research shows that a strong sales culture enhances individual and organizational performance. A strong culture refers to the degree of influence cultural values and norms have on individuals in the organization. The stronger a sales culture, the more individuals will conform to the culture and abide by the norms and values guiding behavior and decision making. Several studies identify relationships between a strong culture and various performance indicators, suggesting that a more influential culture indeed improves individual and business performance. These performance indicators include the following:

- *Satisfaction.* Churchill, Ford, and Walker (1990) found that organizations with more widely shared cultural values experience more positive job satisfaction. That is, a strong culture with clear values that are well communicated increases the likelihood that salespeople will be satisfied with their job.
- *Commitment.* In another study, Mowday, Steers, and Porter (1979) found that when sales cultures are strong, salespeople are more likely to demonstrate commitment to the company and stay in their job for a longer period of time.
- *Turnover.* According to Mobley (1982), a strong sales culture will result in selecting and recruiting salespeople with values that more closely conform to the cultural values of the organization. The findings suggest that this will lead to lower turnover.
- *Performance.* Futrell and Parasuraman (1984) found that there is a positive relationship between the strength of

shared cultural values and sales performance in terms of revenue generated.

- *Role clarification.* A strong culture involving high levels of shared values was found by Behrman and Perreault (1984) to inhibit role ambiguity. According to this argument, clearly communicated values, norms, and beliefs improve access to pertinent information and generally reduce the degree to which information is lacking within the sales organization. This facilitates teaming within the organization, thus leading to more efficient and effective outcomes.

- *Motivation.* Tied closely to performance and commitment, Kohli (1985) found a positive relationship between a strong, well-managed sales culture and motivation among salespeople. A strong culture provides salespeople with direction and an understanding of what needs to be done, thereby motivating them to succeed. Recognition and rewards are provided to support performance expectations that are aligned with the cultural values and norms.

A clear, well-articulated sales culture that effectively influences behaviors and attitudes of employees is more likely to lead to happier salespeople and, consequently, better performing salespeople. Many of the organizations we met with confirmed these research findings with experiences in their own organizations. Motivated, loyal, hard-working, and successful sales professionals result from a culture that strongly influences its members—in other words, those with compelling values, symbols, and supporting practices. Next we discuss how organizations go about creating influential cultures.

HOW SUCCESSFUL ORGANIZATIONS CREATE SALES CULTURES

Successful sales organizations understand why it's important to have an influential culture and how to create the symbols, language, activities, and values to establish positive cultures that win sales. They consciously do things to build and maintain strong sales cultures. Throughout our interviews with leading sales organizations, we observed various best practices that organizations pursue to strengthen their sales culture. As organizations all begin with some type of culture, it is critical that the sales organization create and perpetuate a strong set of cultural norms and values that lead to improved sales performance. Indeed, creating and maintaining a culture is an important strategic effort in and of itself. Following are the critical success factors that leading sales organizations consider when pursuing a strategy to build a culture.

Influence and Fit

A well-managed sales force culture is strong, focused, and appropriate for its environment. That is, it has a high level of influence and direction and it fits the circumstances of the company. The influence of a culture, as discussed in the previous section, depends on how many shared values there are, the extent of sharing, and the prioritization or ordering of those values.

The direction and fit of the culture means that the values and beliefs that constitute the culture are right for the nature of the business and the overall organizational and market environment. Although there is no intrinsically right or wrong work style or culture, the culture must be appropriate for a particular situation—that is, it must be appropriate for the firm's products, markets, selling environment, industry practices, philosophy of management team, and the like.

Some of the environmental factors organizations must account for when developing a culture and creating reinforcing tools, such as recruitment practices, incentive programs, language, and symbols, include:

- Customer buying behavior
- Customer demographics
- Behavior and strategy of competition
- Nature of product or service offerings
- Industry concentration (number of buyers and sellers)

The focus of the sales culture must fit with the company's strategy and the nature of its business. Does the culture guide the type of behaviors and decision making that best suits what's being sold, the type of customers targeted, and the strategic goals of the organization? For example, the "boiler room" cultures of many brokerages in the 1990s did not "fit" well with the new realities of an increasing number of average consumers trading stocks who were turned off by the aggressive, hard-sales tactics of many brokerage firms. At another company participating in our study, salespeople are not commissioned, but rather they work on straight salary and consequently work in teams instead of competing with each other. Teamwork is an important attribute in this company's culture. Because salespeople work in teams with a concentrated number of very large customers across multiple channels, commissioning salespeople would have provided incentives to compete internally where the goals are to work together to grow sales for the company, not for the salesperson.

Compatible Strategies

The company's strategy is both a manifestation of and an influence on the culture. A sales strategy involves a clear understanding about what segment of customers to target, what value is provided to these customers, and how products and services are sold to the marketplace (see Chapter 2 for a more detailed discussion about company strategy). The sales strategy thus focuses and guides all sales efforts and tactics.

The sales culture directs the strategy because the culture is what a company is all about. It also reinforces the implementation of strategy because a strong culture enables an understanding of the strategy and encourages support among employees and a belief that these are the right strategies to pursue, or are at least worthy of support. In order for one of the organizations interviewed for this study to roll out a new customer relationship management (CRM) strategy, management needed to align the culture of the salespeople with the requirements of the strategy. Many of the salespeople were more tenured and used to working with the same systems and processes for many years, and consequently, somewhat resistant to change. By focusing on cultural values that included progressive thinking, technological change, and customer focus, the company was able to demonstrate the benefits of the CRM system and create an acceptance, if not an excitement, among its salespeople about adopting the new system.

Vision

Culture requires a vision of how norms, values, and work behaviors must be so they are aligned with the requirements of the company's current product line, selling environment, and business model. The mission and vision of the company is really a statement of the culture in terms of what the company does, what it aspires to be, and how it will get there. For a culture to be influential, it is critical that company leaders be able to articulate a clear mission and vision for the company. For example, Yellow Book USA has a clear vision and mission: To help small businesses, the engine of the U.S. economy, be successful and increase their sales by providing high-value, low-cost advertising. Everything the sales organization does is guided by this vision and salespeople expressed their pride in providing a service that helps small businesses succeed.

Aligning Organizational Practices at Marriott

The culture at Marriott can be characterized as highly sales- and customer-focused with a significant emphasis on the human element in business regarding both employees and customers. The underlying values and philosophy of the company are underscored by even the most senior leaders and are reflected in many of the processes within the sales organization. At Marriott, everyone knows that "everyone sells" and the customer is highly valued. In fact, Bill Marriott himself makes it a practice to talk with a customer every day.

The processes and policies around teams, training, and recruitment at Marriott are aligned with and support the culture. The company utilizes team strategies to support the culture by creating core teams that are permanently assembled to manage customer relationships, and extended teams as needed to handle specific opportunities.

In-depth sales training programs also support the culture. The company believes that it is important to "train to retain," and the field sales unit is involved in on-the-job training by deploying segment teams that educate the properties on how to obtain business in specific areas, such as government or aviation, so that properties can uncover new sources of business, fill gaps, and sell inventory.

The use of mentoring and recruitment to support the culture is pervasive across the organization. Sales managers have a specific curriculum designed to help them "motivate, inspire, mentor, build customer relationships, and reinforce skills." Finally, Marriott's recruitment policies perpetuate the customer-focused sales culture. Marriott hires predominantly from within those who already possess the key product knowledge and enthusiasm to advance. As a result, tenure tends to be high within the organization and turnover low as the company experiences favorable employee satisfaction and retention.

Communication

Culture requires communication to disseminate stated values, norms, and work standards. Communication, both internal and external, can take place through mottos, public statements, slogans, and other language. Everyone within a sales organization takes part in communicating a culture. Sales managers communicate the culture through mentoring, coaching, daily interactions, training, and events, such as national meetings. According to one sales manager, "Culture even gets down to the language—we use training to establish a common language." Other communications are facilitated by salespeople themselves through such things as sales stories, legends, myths, and real case studies that illustrate the outcomes of the culture.

In one company interviewed, communications that reinforce the culture include a monthly newsletter, which recognizes leading salespeople for the month, and a weekly team meeting that reinforces sales messages and campaigns. At another company, different salespeople on the team leave a voice mail to the whole team about a success story, best practice, or lesson learned that relates in some way to the mission and vision of the company.

MANAGEMENT AS A CULTURAL GUIDE

Organizational leaders not only model the culture, they are responsible for designing policies and procedures that are aligned with and reinforce the underlying culture of the organization. The sales culture is then shaped by the decisions made by sales management regarding training, recruitment, performance measures, incentives, rewards, and recognitions, and the overall structure of the sales force.

Sales training defines the skills and knowledge that are required to meet individual and business performance targets.

Training also helps define and perpetuate a culture because it offers a shared learning experience. Salespeople go through various training program levels in their career learning the ropes with their colleagues. This shared experience is important in the socialization process. Additionally, the content of the training with respect to company policies, procedures, expected behaviors, dos and don'ts, and the like, define the norms and values that compose the sales culture. Unlike employees in other departments of the company, salespeople most often come in contact with their own salespeople with little cross-functional interaction on a day-to-day basis. Sales training then is an important mechanism in building and perpetuating culture.

Many of the organizations we met with said that recruiting the "right" people was one of the more important responsibilities of management to support the culture. Selection criteria, profiles, and testing are a few of the many recruitment tools that organizations utilize to ensure they are picking the people that will best "fit" the culture. By creating a profile of a successful salesperson and a series of requirements and interview items, one participating organization was able to target sales candidates that best fit their cultural mold. If teamwork is an important cultural attribute of a sales force, recruiting the competitive rouge may lead to a bad fit. The culture dictates and at the same time reinforces the kind of person the firm wants to attract.

Selecting the right people and training them helps to facilitate the belief systems and organizational context of the culture. Managers also can guide behavior, decision making, and everyday activities through establishing performance criteria and incentives to perform. Clear standards regarding how salespeople should behave and measuring those standards defines what salespeople are expected to do, what they will be held accountable for, and what they should regard as important—all critical factors required for a strong and successful sales culture. As well, establishing performance standards and incentive programs aligned with the culture helps to monitor salespeople's comprehension of the values being disseminated and rewards them for conforming to the culture.

Sales cultures become more effective as more members of the culture conform to the values and norms. Measuring performance against cultural standards will ensure that individuals understand how they should behave and what is expected of them. Measuring the sales performance of cultural-driven activities, along with recognition and reward systems that provide incentives to conform to cultural standards, will lead to more influential cultures.

Incentives, such as reward and recognition, reinforce what's important as well by defining success and demonstrating how the organization recognizes accomplishment. Individuals like to be rewarded and recognized for performing well and respond in such a way that they continue to try to meet and exceed expectations of performance. In this way, incentives, however they are defined, are important tools that managers use for building strong sales cultures. As one company undergoing a culture change noted, "The first step to changing the culture was measuring productivity, changing compensation, holding salespeople accountable, and documenting and addressing both good and bad performance."

Finally, managers define a culture by how they structure or segment the sales organization. Organizational design—putting people in different positions with different responsibilities—defines the organization's priorities regarding its focus on effectiveness or efficiency, customer targets, allocation of resources, and overall sales strategies.

BEST PRACTICES AND LESSONS LEARNED

Although the organizations we interviewed had different cultures in many respects, all shared certain values. Leading sales organizations seek to create a cultural environment where salespeople are treated with respect and there is an opportunity to grow professionally and personally. Other positive cultural attributes seem so obvious that some organizations take them for granted and fail to develop policies to sustain them. As one new sales leader commented, "I came into an organization that did not have a sales culture at all. People had no selling skills to speak of, and there were no performance metrics in place. The very first thing I did was to create some measures, define processes, and make sure everyone understood what was required from their role." Successful organizations realize that they must be proactive in improving their culture. One company representative noted, "Our culture is our weakness. We are too resistant to change and too entrenched in the past. We gotta get to the other side of the fence."

Without support mechanisms, such as established channels of communication, training programs, incentives, or performance standards, many of these healthy cultural characteristics fall by the wayside. The list of positive attributes might include such things as "having the ability to think for yourself," "being able to see the end results of your work," "being well informed," and "having challenging work."

Similarly, there are negative cultural attributes that can create dissention within a sales force and ultimately lead to employee dissatisfaction and poor performance. For example, treating people differently or unfairly, or showing favoritism, will likely undermine strategic objectives by pitting salespeople against each other. Gossiping, bad-mouthing the company or management, and unhealthy competition that creates an every-person-for-themselves environment creates winners and losers and undermines cultures, or perpetuates bad ones.

One of the most critical aspects of building and maintaining a strong culture is that management models the culture and communicates the cultural values, norms, and expectations in a consistent manner. Cultures fail to influence when there is a disparity between management's stated values and management's actions. However, management can't lead by fear or manipulation, and enforcing a "mandated" culture won't work.

Another important lesson learned is that organizations change and values change. Consequently, the values of a sales culture should be evaluated on a regular basis and updated if necessary, given changes in key personnel, mergers or acquisitions, or a change in the product offerings or customer mix. In particular, organizations that are acquired or merge with organizations that have very different cultures need to evaluate how they can best develop a new culture and reinforce that culture in light of the goals and objectives of the new organization. While this can be a difficult task that involves egos, emotions, and strongly held beliefs, a strategy for creating an influential culture is a requirement for winning sales in today's marketplace.

Marrying Cultures at Stora Enso

The North American operations of Stora Enso is a result of a 1998 merger of Stora and Enso and an acquisition of Consolidated Paper in 2000. Each of the three original companies that formed the new Stora Enso had their own unique history and sales culture: Stora, a Swedish company founded in 1288, was Sweden's oldest surviving mining charter; Enso, incorporated in Finland, had an equally long history; and Consolidated Paper, the Wisconsin-based forestry product company that was originally incorporated in 1894.

The integration of three cultures was seen as both a strength and a challenge for the organization. The culture of the people, management style, and the overall sales culture of each company differed significantly. This made it difficult for salespeople thrown together with very different cultural values, norms, and backgrounds.

In addition to bringing together sales associates from three different countries—complete with language, cultural, and historical differences—the primary cultural distinction centered on the hierarchical versus decentralized nature of the organization and decision-making authority. Stora was traditionally a flat organization with a decentralized decision-making authority, meaning that salespeople were empowered to make decisions in the field without being required to seek approval from their managers. Enso was more of a hierarchical organization, and Consolidated Paper's culture was characterized as a traditional U.S. manufacturing top-down, decision-making organization with a very centralized authority. In both Enso and Consolidated, salespeople were not accustomed to making their own decisions in the field.

The new Stora Enso culture adopted various attributes from each of the three legacy companies. This new hybrid culture, while borrowing from the Enso and Consolidated cultures, tended to give more weight to the flat, decentralized authority structure of Stora. Consequently, various individuals throughout the organization, depending on the company they came from, had challenges with adapting to new and unfamiliar leadership styles. Some salespeople were not comfortable with making decisions on their own, while others were not comfortable with having to consult with their manager before making decisions in the field.

The company has made great strides in creating a new and distinct sales culture, and through training its salespeople have become "more culturally diverse and aware in their thought processes and more open-minded and accepting of different cultures." They are also more comfortable with knowing when to make autonomous decisions and when to report to management.

9

CUSTOMERS' DEMANDS
FOR MORE
Buying Behaviors and Attitudes

"Buyers want their suppliers to make life simpler for them. They say, 'Show me real productivity gains in a simple way that won't burden my IT shop; don't promise me the world.'"

—Sales Manager

Customers today may be more demanding than ever. With the information available to them on the Internet and the growing efforts among organizations to improve customer service, customers have not only come to expect more from suppliers, but they are more knowledgeable, more sophisticated, and more price sensitive. It has indeed become a buyer's market, and the increasing leverage held by customers is putting unprecedented pressures on suppliers and leading to increased competition, lower prices, lower margins, and sales organizations scrambling to differentiate themselves in the marketplace.

Sales organizations have caught on to the customer-focused movement by pursuing many of the organizational and technological strategies discussed in this book. For some of these organizations, however, their efforts to better serve customers are guided by their own ideas of what their customers value and how those customers prefer to buy. Even with elaborate customer service data-gathering techniques, figuring out what customers want is not easy, and their true preferences are not always observable or predictable.

Industry- or organizational-level changes among customers, such as consolidation, use of buying committees or electronic reverse auctions, and other "buying practices," may be spotted fairly easily, but more team- and individual-level attitudinal changes in how and why customers buy can be far more difficult for sales organizations to pin down. For example, customers' perceptions of relationships, what they value from suppliers, what they value or don't value in their salesperson, and what drives their buying decisions, change often and are difficult to track.

This chapter attempts to paint a more complete picture of customers' preferences and buying practices by identifying what they want, how they buy, and how that's changing at the industry, company, and buyer levels. We look specifically at the changes in the behaviors and attitudes of customers as observed by the leading organizations interviewed for our study and compare them with findings from our survey study of customer buying behaviors and attitudes. This study, a survey of more than 500 buyers of information technology (IT) from small and medium-sized organizations across a wide variety of industries, attempts to shed light on what customers value most in their supplier, how they prefer to buy, where they prefer to buy, and what most influences their decision to buy or not to buy. This chapter reports the findings from this survey study to compare what sales organizations think customers want to what customers actually say they want from their salesperson and vendor organization. Reconciling what customers want with what and how salespeople deliver their products and services has important strategic implications for a sales organization's ability to win over smarter and more demanding customers.

CUSTOMERS WANT MORE OF EVERYTHING

The leading sales organizations we interviewed shared with us their observations of how customers are changing the way they buy, and the challenges customers present in terms of being able to meet their needs, provide value, create relationships, and ultimately grow sales. In this section, we review the changes taking place among customers as perceived by sales organizations, with the objective of highlighting the most significant changes in the marketplace that successful organizations must address. We'll also draw comparisons of these observations with what customers actually had to say about their buying behaviors and what they value most and least in their salespeople.

Customers Know More and Expect More

Customers are more knowledgeable, more sophisticated in terms of how they make buying decisions, and ultimately more demanding of suppliers. They expect the same level of service regardless of channel, and with access to information about products and pricing on the Internet, they expect to get the best deal possible from their suppliers. These trends among customers hold true for all of the organizations we interviewed, from those selling yellow pages advertising to those selling large enterprisewide networking systems.

For example, small business customers of BellSouth have changed significantly in the past few years both in their buying behaviors and knowledge of technology. With an increase in the number of telecommunications providers, small business customers have been able to significantly increase their knowledge of both technology offerings and pricing. According to the company, customers understand technology and are less inclined to look at long-term contracts because they know they will have a lot of choices in the future because technology changes so rapidly. Even smaller customers are more technologically competent than in the past. According to one manager at BellSouth, it "used to be that customers were just happy if they picked up the phone and had a dial tone. Now they are concerned about other issues like wireless capabilities or disaster recovery systems."

Organizations such as TD Waterhouse that are in business-to-consumer (B2C) markets are also experiencing more demanding and knowledgeable customers. According to the company, "Customers are generally more sophisticated and intelligent when it comes to equity research, product knowledge, and balancing portfolios." One company from the automotive industry said their customers have a sharper eye for value and are better at gathering information on products. Customers used to go to auto shops to collect information, whereas now they come knowing what they want. Given this new level of expertise, customers are asking sales representatives for more advanced information on product features, which requires salespeople to be on top of any product changes. Another company we interviewed noted that with customers becoming more knowledgeable through information available on the Web, such things as regional pricing and fulfillment are becoming more difficult.

Finally, customers expect faster service. According to Diebold, one of the leading producers of automated teller machines (ATMs) in the United States, just in the past couple of years, product lead time from contract to delivery has been reduced by two-thirds. Because their customers are building branches more quickly, they expect faster outfitting of ATMs and security systems.

Customers expect more, in part, because their business requirements are becoming more complex. Business today, even for small organizations, is more complicated, and as organizations become more sophisticated, they demand more from their product and service suppliers. Several organizations noted a trend toward increased complexity of contract requirements, including such things as customization of solutions, logistics, and longer-term fulfillment issues. At Marriott International, for example, with declining meeting attendance and tight travel budgets becoming the norm in today's business world, organizers of meetings, conventions, and conferences now require more complex and sophisticated contract negotiations around such parameters as price, guaranteed room nights, locations, and cancellation policies.

Customers Are More Concerned with Price

The organizations we interviewed identified several underlying causes for the dramatic increase in the focus on price among their customers: customers have become more aware of competitive pricing, they understand the financial implications of their purchases, *their* customers are expecting lower prices, and in many industries, products have become commoditized whereby differentiation among competitive offerings has been reduced to price alone. As customers come under greater financial pressures, they are naturally fixated on short-term solutions and this fixation with price carries on throughout the sales cycle.

Office Depot, a leading office equipment supplier to the retail and small business market, said that customers and prospects now more than ever "are singularly focused on per-unit prices." They believe this new cost consciousness "to be a direct reflection of the renewed priority of businesses to operate more profitably on stagnant or declining revenues." Similarly, another company said their customers emphasize price to the extent that they demand multiyear contracts with guaranteed price reductions. Clearly, from the perspective of leading sales organizations, price is an important issue for customers; so important that for many it is the primary driver of their buying decisions.

Another organization characterized the relationship with their customers as "strained at best." The organization relayed how their customers are demanding price concessions with no commitment to buy, and are employing tactics to inhibit relationships with their suppliers. Getting beat up on price and reducing the ability of the sales force to establish important relationships with suppliers are just a couple of examples where customers are leveraging their power over suppliers to gain price concessions.

Customers Are Buying More at "Arm's Length"

Findings from our study confirm that salespeople are finding it more and more difficult to gain access to buyers. Customers' buying practices are only making it more difficult. Through the use of requests for proposals (RFPs) and electronic auctions, and by assigning buying decisions to "third parties," such as the procurement department or committees or consultants, customers are making it hard for salespeople to get face time with the end user, influence decision makers, and ultimately create lasting relationships with customers.

It was common to hear throughout our interviews about customers using the RFP process, Internet auctions, and other means of arm's-length procurement. One sales representative lamented that the procurement departments of most customers now have ten times the power today than they did four to five years ago. Another company told us that purchasing decisions among their customers are increasingly being made by committees and often managed through a detailed and formalized procurement process. This makes it extremely difficult for sales organizations to show value and differentiate themselves. In the end, products and services are reduced to commodities—forcing competitive bids to focus solely on delivery capability and price.

Diebold has observed the increase in the use of RFPs, which they see as making it more difficult to "be creative" in proposing solutions. According to one manager, "Customers give you RFPs with blanks for the cost . . . sometimes they don't even allow you to make presentations, just fill in the blanks." How to configure the deal and include value-added service or other intangibles is difficult to specify in a fill-in-the-blank RFP form. The general feeling is that unless a salesperson becomes involved with an account prior to the RFP being released, there is a significantly lower chance of winning the sale.

For other organizations, buying decisions today take place at different levels in the client organization than in the past. Decisions are being pushed to higher levels in some instances and to lower levels in others, depending on the product and importance of the sale to the client. According to Office Depot, in the past it was purchasers who were generally mid- to lower-level ranking individuals with minimal accountability to their organization that were assigned the responsibility of purchasing "pens and pencils." Now, the company is seeing more senior-level purchasers, including COOs, CFOs, and company owners, occupying the decision-making chair. To complicate matters, these new decision makers are responsible for much more than purchasing office supplies, so getting their attention can be a major hurdle.

Reverse auctions or electronic auctions take place when a buyer electronically posts a notice to buy a product or service. The request includes product and delivery requirements and sometimes even price limits. Selected vendors will then participate in a bidding war online and in real time, with the contract generally going to the lowest bidder. This is becoming a popular practice in some industries because it's a cheap and expedient way for customers to do business. Stora Enso, Marriott, Infineum, and Hewlett Packard (HP) are a few of the organizations we studied that have encountered reverse electronic auctions. While they normally take place for traditional commodities, this practice is emerging in some service and high-tech, complex product areas. The phenomenon reflects the commoditization of products and services, the focus on price, and ultimately the customer's desire for faster and easier business transactions.

More Customers Are Consolidating

As the rate of mergers and acquisitions is growing and organizations leverage the strategic benefits of partnerships, more customers both large and small are consolidating. We found this to be the case across nearly all industries studied. Consolidation of customers increases their buying power while offering fewer, albeit larger, opportunities for suppliers. The organizations interviewed observed that while some consolidation within the customer marketplace meant that there were bigger contracts to be won, more often than not the increasing buying leverage resulting from fewer and larger customers presented challenges for their sales strategies.

Infineum, the manufacturer of fuel and lubricant additives, reports that their customers have become "bigger and more globalized." The company notes that consolidation began with their largest customers, but is expected to continue among the mid-sized organizations as well. In response, Infineum has had to develop strategies to win the big accounts and then meet their needs in different parts of the world. Finally, a wave of merger and acquisitions among Diebold's customers over the past several years has created a small number of very large financial services institutions, substantially reducing the number of middle-tier banks Diebold can sell to. This consolidation in both supply and demand will likely continue as cost pressures and slimmer margins make it more difficult for organizations going it alone to remain competitive. In today's competitive global economy, buying power, access to more markets, and economies of scale are all in the favor of organizations that merge, acquire, or partner in some way.

How Salespeople Are Responding

Sales organizations have adopted various strategies to overcome these challenges and address the increasing leverage customers are gaining vis-à-vis sellers. As discussed in previous chapters, many of the salespeople interviewed stressed the importance of creating relationships for overcoming these challenges, becoming Trusted Advisors, and increasing the value they provide to customers by offering more business and product knowledge.

Salespeople told us they feel that creating lasting and meaningful relationships with customers is critical for winning their business in this new selling environment. Becoming a trusted business advisor to their clients would allow them to recommend the best solutions to their business challenges and thus increase customer retention over time. Similarly, providing value through offering detailed product and service information and demonstrating how those products and services result in strategic benefits for the customer would help reinforce relationships, circumvent arm's-length buying practices, satisfy price concerns, and ultimately meet customers' demands for more. As part of our survey study about what buyers want, how they buy, and why they buy, we sought to compare what sales organizations are trying to do to win customers with what customers say will win their business.

WHAT CUSTOMERS WANT
AND HOW THEY BUY

Leading sales organizations know that it's important to have a finger on the pulse of what customers want and value. They do this through satisfaction and loyalty studies, customer service calls, and merely by having salespeople in the field probing for customers' preferences, motivations, and future buying patterns. This information is critical to developing strategies for improving the customer experience and establishing long-term relationships—the goal of all sales organizations in today's competitive marketplace.

This book has primarily been about the efforts of organizations to build strategies that win sales and the data from the research presented throughout has been from the seller's perspective. Following the completion of our in-depth interviews, we conducted a survey study that focused on buying attitudes and practices from the perspective of customers—in this case, buyers of information technology (IT) products and services. We focused our investigation on buyers from a very large and important segment of the economy—small and medium-sized businesses—and across all industries that purchase IT products and services. Focusing on this industry segment for the survey study provided a good comparison with the organizations we interviewed for the larger study because many of those organizations deal with IT products and services in one way or another. And because most leading sales organizations we surveyed are engaged in primarily business-to-business (B2B) transactions, examining business buyers allows us to make some interesting comparisons between the two studies. Even though this was a B2B study, there are some interesting lessons here for B2C salespeople as well.

The survey study asked buyers to discuss what is important to them when buying technology from vendors and their salespeople, what they look for and value in vendors, how they purchase from a behavioral standpoint—their buying process—and how they feel about buying through alternative channels. Buyers were then asked to think about what they value in salespeople, what characteristics of salespeople influence their decision to buy or not to buy, and how they would describe their own salespeople. These findings shed light on buyers' attitudes and buying practices and will provide sales organizations a valuable perspective when developing strategies to win sales.

Why Do Customers Buy?

Leading sales organizations know that customers will buy when they require a solution to a business challenge or seek to improve the effectiveness or efficiency in the way they conduct their business. Understanding precisely why customers buy and what their needs are is critical information for salespeople because their chances of making a sale are improved if their product or service solution provides the best fit for the client's need.

Customers of IT from small and medium-sized businesses were asked to select the three most important motivating factors for buying new technology. As Figure 9.1 shows, not surprisingly, customers most often buy new technology to "increase productivity"—that is, to produce more at lower costs. Slightly more than half buy new technology to "cut costs" related to operations, and nearly half said they buy new technology to "bet-

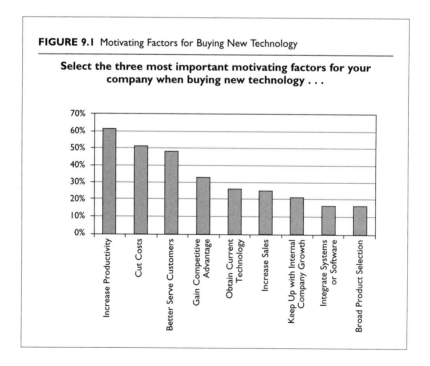

FIGURE 9.1 Motivating Factors for Buying New Technology

ter serve customers." The data validate the belief among sales organizations that customers buy products and services most often to increase the value they can offer to their customers at a lower cost to them. This emphasizes the importance of the business issue selling model indicating that salespeople need to understand what impacts their customers' productivity and what their customers need to better serve their marketplace.

Just about one-quarter of all buyers said they buy to "obtain current technology," 25 percent said they buy to "increase sales," and just 21 percent buy new technology to "keep up with internal company growth." Clearly, this is valuable information to sales organizations that must focus their sales efforts on the real needs of customers. Moreover, accounting for customers' pain points and buying triggers in the customer relationship process will guide salespeople in the right direction when they interact with their customers.

In high-performing sales organizations, salespeople typically spend a considerable amount of time researching their prospects' needs before making sales calls, and their customer resource management (CRM) or sales force automation (SFA) systems provide important tools for better managing (and documenting) the needs of their customers. These findings suggest that customers' most important needs are to be more efficient and effective in serving their own customers. Successful sales organizations know this and they build it in to their sales strategies.

Who Do Customers Buy From and How?

One important aspect of understanding customers' buying behaviors is being able to identify customers' channel preferences. What is the propensity of customers to purchase from a salesperson versus a Web site? When and why do customers go directly through a vendor as opposed to a reseller, distributor, or other channel partner?

We asked IT buyers how they most often buy various technologies and what channels they are most likely to purchase through. According to our survey, nearly half of all buyers purchased their IT products or services through a salesperson, 40 percent purchased via online, and 11 percent bought through other channels. The salesperson today is competing then for half of all of customers' purchases. As that proportion continues to decline, organizations will need to ensure that their salespeople are relevant for their customers. Later in the chapter we will explore more closely what it means to be relevant and valuable from the customers' perspective.

Figure 9.2 breaks down the most frequent purchases by channels for seven IT product/service areas. Except for PCs and laptops, which are generally commodities, technology products and services are purchased most often through a salesperson because they are typically more complex and may involve significant customization and unique customer requirements. Of those technologies, customers are most likely to buy telecommunications voice/data services through salespeople (70 percent) with only 24 percent buying through a Web site. This is followed by new telecommunications products and services and

FIGURE 9.2 Breakdown of IT Purchases by Channel

In most instances, how do you buy the following technologies?

Channel	Voice/ Data	New Telecom.	Network Equip.	PCs/ Laptops
Web Site	24%	30%	48%	57%
Salesperson	70	64	46	38
Other	6	6	6	5

Channel	Servers	Mobile Devices	Software	All
Web Site	50%	45%	37%	40%
Salesperson	44	44	48	49
Other	6	14	15	11

software. Slightly more than half of purchases involving PCs/laptops and servers are made on the Web.

Buying online is no longer solely a B2C transaction as business buyers are seeing the benefits of purchasing online. A study conducted by Forrester Research (2003) examined the usage of e-commerce by buyers from four industries (business and consumer services, manufacturing, retail, and financial services). More than half of buyers from the services industry said they purchase through e-commerce channels, followed by 46 percent of manufacturers, 38 percent of retail, and 33 percent of financial services.

In addition to their own sales channels, many organizations now sell through third-party channels, presenting even more competition for the sales force. Our study further investigated third-party channel preferences among customers for a wide variety of IT products and services. When asked what sales channel buyers are most likely to purchase through, exactly half prefer to buy IT directly from the vendor or service provider. Only about 15 percent buy through a vendor's channel partner, and 13 percent most often purchase IT through resellers. IT customers from small and medium-sized businesses buy technology from a retail store around 10 percent of the time and from a third-party consultant 4 percent of the time. Sales organizations that understand their customers' preferences are able to leverage high-value channels and allocate the appropriate resources according to channel usage. Because all customers will not prefer the same channel for all products, accurately identifying the mix of channel usage by buyer preference and product type, although tricky, is important for ensuring that the right resources and skills are dedicated to the right places.

Hewlett Packard is one such company that understands channel selection and preference among its customers. They know that if customers are buying desktops and notebooks they will likely prefer call center support with easy fulfillment. But there are also those who look to HP to have a consultative role

Adapting to Customer Changes at TD Waterhouse

When the stock market's high-flying glory days of the 1990s abruptly ended, individual investors changed the way they bought and sold equities. During that stock market bubble, many consumers—sensing they couldn't lose—conducted their own research and did their own buying and selling of stocks. Many quit their jobs and became day traders. Today, however, "customers are more cautious in their trading and they are looking for more conservative investments and better advice," said one TD Waterhouse manager. Customers are generally more sophisticated and intelligent when it comes to equity research, so they expect their financial service providers to make the research available but also to be there when they need help or advice.

TD Waterhouse recognizes that customers are now looking for more services, more advice, and better customer service, whether they want to trade themselves or rely on the company's expert brokers. More demanding customers mean the company's associates must raise their level of professionalism and knowledge and be able to more quickly recognize the needs of customers. The company has conducted training to ensure that their brokers are meeting customers' needs where they want to conduct their transactions—whether it is online or with a real-life broker.

in their business and they will go through the direct sales force. HP also knows which customers and what types of customers will typically purchase through value-added resellers (VARs) so that they can manage that channel appropriately.

Customers' Buying Practices

Based on marketplace trends we identified through our interviews with the world's leading sales organizations, we also developed a list of behaviors and attitudes to validate such trends with customers of IT products and services in the small and medium-sized business market. Buyers were asked to rate a series of statements based on their organization's buying practices. The results suggest that although price is important, in general, customers really want a supplier who is easy to do business with—one who provides good service and after-sales support.

Figure 9.3 shows the percent of buyers who agree or strongly agree with each buying practice. Next to the column with the percentages is a column containing the mean score for each practice based on a five-point scale. Although a majority of buyers agree that "price is one of the most important factors," more buyers agree or strongly agree that they "will pay a premium for excellent after-sales service." This suggests that price matters, but it's secondary to service after the sale.

Half of all of those surveyed "buy online when possible," again reinforcing accounts that more customers today have a propensity to purchase through that channel. Just 44 percent agree or strongly agree with the statement that they "prefer to buy from one rather than multiple suppliers." This seems to validate several observations made during our interviews that many customers are moving toward outsourcing to more rather than fewer vendors.

FIGURE 9.3 Customers' Buying Practices

Please rate the following statements about your company's buying behavior . . .

Buying Practice	Agree/ Strongly Agree	Mean Score
I will pay a premium for excellent after-sales service.	67%	3.64
Price is one of the most important factors.	64	3.54
I buy online when possible.	50	3.39
I prefer to buy from one rather than multiple suppliers.	44	3.28
I will pay a premium if a vendor has competent salespeople.	30	2.83
I frequently use request for proposals (RFPs).	29	2.79

Customers also were asked to rate their agreement with the statement "I will pay a premium if a vendor has competent salespeople." It appears that price is more important than having a good salesperson as only 30 percent of buyers agree or strongly agree with that statement. The mean of 2.83 suggests that respondents were even less than neutral on this practice, scoring more disagrees and strongly disagrees. In the end, we can conclude from the data that while price is very important, even more important than a "competent salesperson," it is not as critical as "excellent after-sales service." These findings reinforce the overarching theme that customers want suppliers who are easy to do business with.

Finally, only 29 percent agree or strongly agree that they "frequently use request for proposals (RFPs)." This is not surprising given the size of the businesses that participated in the survey. Generally speaking, larger organizations are more likely to utilize RFPs than small and medium-sized organizations because formal purchasing policies and budget and approval processes are more common among larger organizations.

What Customers Value in Suppliers

In addition to understanding how customers buy, it is also important for organizations to identify what they can do to increase value for the customer and, consequently, what the sales force should focus on when interacting with customers.

IT buyers were asked to rate the importance of vendor characteristics in their decision to buy from a supplier. Once again, service rises to the top. As Figure 9.4 shows, three-quarters felt that "service reputation" is a very or extremely important characteristic when selecting a vendor, followed by "product reputation" and "financial stability." Although salespeople do not directly control these factors, especially the company's financial health, indirectly they can influence service and product reputation through each and every interaction they have with a client.

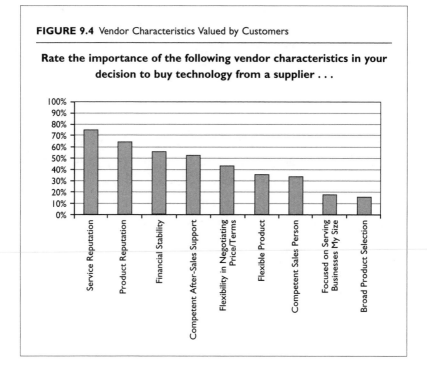

FIGURE 9.4 Vendor Characteristics Valued by Customers

Rate the importance of the following vendor characteristics in your decision to buy technology from a supplier . . .

The importance of service is further reinforced by the fact that more buyers said that "competent after-sales support" is more important than "flexibility in negotiating price/term" and "flexible product," and far more important than a "competent salesperson."

Clearly, sales competency, product selection, and flexibility in negotiating terms were less important buying triggers than service, support, and product reputation. These findings demonstrate how important it is that salespeople sell customers on their company's ability to service them and the importance of establishing confidence in their brand throughout the marketplace. Instead of guessing, successful sales organizations can learn from their customers about what attributes and characteristics they value most so they can develop sales strategies that focus on improving the critical factors that have the greatest influence on the decision to buy. On an individual level, salespeople must identify ways in which they can impact these more organizational characteristics for the client.

Customers Rely on Salespeople

Salespeople hope that customers depend on them to solve their business problems so that they can become a Trusted Advisor (see Chapter 5), relied on for their consultative, value-added services. The belief that this type of interaction will ultimately strengthen relationships that translate into long-term customers for the sales organization is shared by many of the leading organizations we interviewed. To get the customer's perspective, we asked buyers to select the information topics they relied on their salesperson for as their primary source of information.

As Figure 9.5 shows, customers reported that they did not frequently depend on their salesperson in "identifying strategic IT opportunities for me" (28 percent). Rather, customers said they most relied on their salesperson for "obtaining the best price" (66 percent) and "understanding product features/benefits" (65 percent). Less than a quarter of buyers said they relied on their salesperson when it came to "diagnosing my IT problems" (24 percent).

Finally, the leading sales organizations we interviewed said that many of their customers are increasingly demanding that salespeople be able to demonstrate a return on their investment. The survey study, in contrast, did not bear that out as only 17 percent said they relied on their salesperson for "calculating the return on my investment." One reason for this may be that ROI might not be as important of an issue for IT buyers as other product or service categories.

The results suggest that sales organizations must ensure that their strategies reinforce product knowledge and expertise among the sales force, along with negotiation skills in the sales

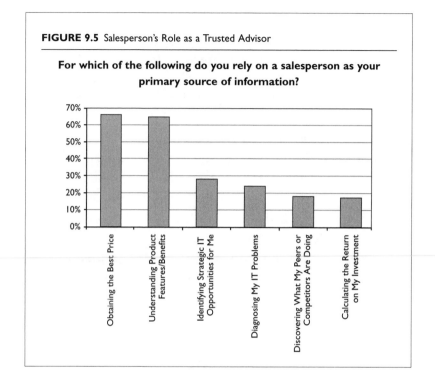

FIGURE 9.5 Salesperson's Role as a Trusted Advisor

For which of the following do you rely on a salesperson as your primary source of information?

and customer relationship process. As well, identifying strategic opportunities and diagnosing problems for the client—that is, selling consultatively—may be important for some customers but not others. Sales organizations must know which is which so that they are not trying to be a trusted business advisor when the customer only wants the best price, or vice versa.

Characteristics of Salespeople That Influence Buying Decisions

Purchasing decisions are influenced to one degree or another by a customer's interactions with their salesperson. Leading sales organizations understand that deals can be made or lost as a result of how their salespeople interact with customers, so they develop carefully planned account management strategies and customer relationship processes that are predicated on the company's perception of what customers value. However, organizations are not always successful in identifying what has the greatest influence on buying decisions. As sales organizations develop strategies for creating lasting relationships with customers and adding value to each interaction, it is important to first understand, on the salesperson-customer level, the key factors of that relationship affecting customers' decisions to buy.

A common belief among sales organizations, as one sales manager described, is that "customers value relationships, they expect their salesperson to understand their business, and they expect honesty." We questioned customers about what they actually value in their salesperson and what behaviors of their salesperson influence their decision to buy or not to buy.

Customers were asked to list the three most important attributes of a salesperson that influenced their decision to purchase from that salesperson. The characteristics evaluated in the study were phrased in either a negative or a positive way, depending on whether it was a factor deterring or facilitating a purchase. The first column in Figure 9.6 ranks negative characteristics of salespeople by the percentage of buyers saying that these characteristics turn them off from buying. These are the characteristics that customers said would kill a deal for them.

According to the survey, customers said they are most likely to not buy from a salesperson who is "dishonest" (59 percent), who "doesn't know product" (54 percent), or who is "unresponsive/doesn't follow up" (48 percent). Forty-four percent said that "pushy" salespeople will kill the deal for them, followed by "doesn't listen well" (28 percent)—note the significant drop-off placed on the importance of characteristics leading buyers to not purchase.

The top three characteristics customers said would make them not buy are the same three mentioned as those most influencing customers to buy, although they're in a different order of

importance. Nearly the same percentage of buyers said "respon-
sive/follows up" and "honest" were characteristics that were
equally as important for winning or losing a deal. One significant difference in the top three, however, is product knowledge.
While 54 percent said that a salesperson that "doesn't know
product" would make them decide not to buy, 71 percent said
that "knows product" would make them decide to buy. Clearly,
product knowledge is more important for influencing customers to buy than making them decide not to buy—that is, a salesperson with product knowledge is more likely to win a deal
than the lack of product knowledge is likely to lose a deal.

As mentioned, many salespeople we interviewed believed
that to keep customers they needed to be friendly, create relationships, and understand the customer's business. Customers,
however, rated these characteristics as much less important factors in their decision to not buy. Only 13 percent said they
would not buy because their salesperson is "unfriendly," 12 percent said that salespeople viewing the "sale as transaction" would
turn them off from buying, and 11 percent would not buy from
a salesperson who had "no experience in my industry." These
characteristics are not likely to kill a deal, but how important
are they for winning a deal?

Having "no experience in my industry" was twice as important for making customers decide to buy than not to buy, and
"views sale as relationship" was also more important for motivating decisions to buy than not to buy. However, being "friendly"
(8 percent) had little influence on decisions to buy or not to
buy. This supports the notion that professional relationships
based on expertise and trust are more valuable to customers
than personal relationships based on friendliness.

In addition to "experience in my industry" and the manner
in which the salesperson views sales interactions, "understands
my business" was also more important for winning deals than
losing deals. Nearly half said that a salesperson who "understands my business" would lead them to buy, while just about

FIGURE 9.6 Salesperson Characteristics Affecting Customer Decision to Purchase

What three characteristics or behaviors of a salesperson make you decide . . .

not to buy from that salesperson?		to buy from that salesperson?	
Dishonest	59%	Knows Product	71%
Does Not Know Product	54	Honest	55
Unresponsive/No Follow-up	48	Responsive/Follows-Up	46
Pushy	44	Understands My Business	46
Does Not Listen Well	28	Experience In My Industry	23
Doesn't Understand My Business	26	Views Sale As Relationship	23
Unfriendly	13	Listens Well	22
Views Sale As Transaction	12	Friendly	8
No Experience In My Industry	11	Persistent	1

one in four said that "doesn't understand my business" would make them not buy.

Finally, a salesperson who "doesn't listen well" is more likely to turn off a buyer than a salesperson who "listens well" is likely to win a sale. "Pushy" (44 percent) is an important factor for losing deals, but someone who is seen as "persistent" (1 percent) matters little for making a decision to buy.

Understanding what to do and what not to do can make or break a sale. At the least, salespeople need to be honest, know their products, and be responsive in dealing with the customer. After that, they should make sure they understand their customer's business but shouldn't be pushy. While honesty and knowledge are critical, customers said that how their salesperson "views sale as relationship" and how "friendly" they are have far less influence on their buying decision.

How Customers View Their Salesperson

As previously mentioned, customers of telecommunications services and products were most likely to purchase from a salesperson compared with other channels. Because buyers of telecom were more likely to interact with a salesperson, we asked them to describe their salesperson using the same descriptors from the previous question regarding important influences on buying decisions. Table 9.7 ranks characteristics of salespeople by the percentage of customers who mentioned those characteristics when describing their salesperson.

Customers generally had good things to say about their salesperson, mentioning positive characteristics more often than negative ones. Overall, customers said that their salesperson possessed the same characteristics that were also most important in influencing their decision to buy (discussed above). Customers most often said that their salesperson "knows the product," is "responsive," and is "honest." Thirty-seven percent said their salesperson was "friendly," although that mattered little in their decision to buy or not to buy as discussed above. More than a third (35 percent) said that their salesperson "listens well," again, however, not especially important for driving a decision to buy.

If sales organizations are implementing strategies to improve "relationship selling" as opposed to selling in transactional terms,

FIGURE 9.7 Salesperson Characteristics as Ranked by Telecommunications Customers

For telecommunications purchases, which of the following characteristics describe your salesperson?

Characteristic		Characteristic, cont'd	
Knows product	52%	Views sale as transaction	8%
Responsive	40	Unresponsive	7
Honest	39	No experience in my industry	5
Friendly	37	Doesn't understand my business	5
Listens well	35	Doesn't listen well	4
Understands my business	32	Pushy	4
Views sale as relationship	27	Doesn't know product	4
Experience in my industry	22	Unfriendly	3
Persistent	9	Dishonest	3

they are doing a pretty good job of it in the telecommunications services and products sector. Approximately 27 percent of IT buyers said that their salesperson for telecommunications products and services "views sale as relationship," while only 8 percent said their salesperson "views sale as transaction." This shows that customers will have different expectations of different types of vendors and salespeople. Those who prefer to buy through a simple transaction, at more of an arm's length, will likely have lower expectations of their vendor than those customers requiring consultation and expert advice for making a purchase.

BEST PRACTICES AND LESSONS LEARNED

Most everyone agrees that customers of all shapes and sizes in today's marketplace are demanding more. They are more sophisticated, more knowledgeable, and more price conscious than perhaps ever before. From even cursory observations it is clear what customers are demanding: They want vendors who are easy to do business with—that is, who provide optimal service—and who provide the services and products that meet their needs.

Naturally, different customers will have different needs, and how they define excellent service will vary, but sales organizations must be able to identify these differences from their customer's point of view, rather than relying on preconceived notions of how sales organizations and salespeople should sell to customers. The sales organization's perspective of what customers value may not always represent what customers say they value. A strategy for identifying and understanding what customers value and how they buy is essential for providing the right solutions through the right type of sales interaction.

The following highlights key outcomes derived from our review of buying behaviors and attitudes from the customers' perspectives and, more importantly, their implications for sales strategies.

More customers value products and services that help their business perform better and increase value to their customers. It seems obvious, but to be successful in today's competitive marketplace, it is critical that sales organizations know why their customers buy. IT customers reported that they buy because they require solutions that will improve the efficiency and effectiveness of their business, and they buy to better serve their customers. Knowing why they buy provides critical data to inform sales strategies, messages, and tactics so that salespeople are able to efficiently tailor solutions that best meet customers' needs.

Customers want their buying experience to be easy and convenient—regardless of the channel. As alternative sales channels both within organizations and through third parties continue to grow in importance, salespeople will need to ensure that they provide the value that customers look for from a direct channel. Customers will go to different channels depending on their needs, but sales organizations must develop strategies that will make sure those needs are met regardless of the channel. While consumers have been the primary Web buyers, business customers will continue to increase their purchases over the Web as this channel becomes more sophisticated and robust in facilitating the buying experience.

For the sales organization, leaders must identify which customers prefer to buy through which channels so that they can allocate resources to each channel in the most effective and cost-efficient manner. For salespeople, it will be important to identify ways they can provide value to the customer beyond what customers get through other channels, such as the Web or resellers. Many nondirect channels look alike, and it's difficult to add any unique value for the customer through these alternative channels. Thus, sales organizations must differentiate themselves through their direct sales force—those that can't figure out how to increase value to the customer provided through their direct channel will become undifferentiated and lose sales to those organizations that can.

Service and product reputation is often more important than price. Ask salespeople what customers are most concerned with and many will tell you "price." While almost always an important issue for everyone involved, customers in our study mentioned other factors that are equally if not more important in their decision to buy. According to the study, customers said they would pay more if they could get excellent after-sales service, and they placed premium value on service and product reputation. In fact, service was the most important factor they valued from their vendor organization.

Sales organizations can't compete or differentiate themselves on price alone. Creating and maintaining an excellent reputation of both service and product should be a primary focus of sales organizations. Salespeople will need to perpetuate that reputation through their behavior in the field and ensure that they instill confidence among customers who have come to expect excellent service and after-sales support.

Some customers rely on salespeople for price and product information, others look for strategic partners. The question for sales organizations is how to identify which customers are merely looking for price and product information and which require a trusted business advisor—and which customers are somewhere in between.

Many sales organizations believe that the best way to be customer-focused is to diagnose their customers' problems, act as strategic consultants, and calculate a return on investment for the customer. However, not all customers may want this. For many, all they want from their salesperson is the ability to negotiate a good price and information on the features and benefits of the product or service they are considering buying. With all of the competing sources of information available to customers, salespeople need to know when a customer relies on them for the simple facts as opposed to solving their strategic business challenges. A strategy for segmenting customers based on buying behavior and needs allows sales organizations to distribute resources in an optimal way.

Customers want more honest, responsive, and knowledgeable salespeople. Salespeople typically emphasize the importance of being friendly, developing relationships, listening well, and being persistent when interacting with customers. However, customers have simply come to expect these behaviors as given and they no longer view them as differentiators in the marketplace. Shouldn't all salespeople be friendly? It may be nice to have a friendly and persistent salesperson, but it's not a requirement.

What customers do require is that their salesperson be honest, responsive to their needs, and diligent in following up when they say they will, as well as knowledgeable about the products. According to customers, these attributes have the most influence on their decision to buy. Sales organizations have to develop policies, incentives, and sales practices to ensure their salespeople are exhibiting these behaviors.

The influence customers have today in the buyer-seller relationship in many industries is what drives the strategies discussed in this book. Clearly, customers have come to expect a high level of service and quality products at the best price. As these expectations cross alternative sales channels, leading organizations have stepped up to meet the challenge. Sales organizations will best differentiate themselves, however, by providing additional value through their direct sales channel, but only for those customers who need additional value and can't get it elsewhere. Knowing who these customers are and what they value will be important to winning sales.

Having a handle on what customers want and value, how they buy, and why they buy is an important step in building strategies that win sales. This information allows sales organizations to best segment their market, appropriately allocate resources across the sales force, implement effective sales tactics, and develop training programs. Ultimately, such strategies of successful sales organizations are geared to meeting the needs of their customers regardless of how simple or complex, and regardless of what channel the transaction comes through.

10

CONCLUSION

"We made [technology] investments and put in metrics and scorecards and a performance management system. We put in hard tools around process and pipeline management and we put in soft tools, such as management coaching and sales training. We resegmented our customers and changed our recruiting profile."

—Sales Leader (describing a three-year window of change)

This final chapter summarizes the strategies detailed throughout this study, discusses the underlying themes among them, and considers how to use the contents of this book within your own business.

SUMMARIZING THE STRATEGIES THAT WIN

While each organization had individual circumstances and operated in discrete industries, all were experiencing similar challenges in the markets in which they operated. These challenges, such as global economies, customer sophistication, and growing competition, were driving their strategies for building and operating their sales organizations. Although these were not necessarily new challenges, and in many cases had been exacerbated by the recent economic downturn, there was a universal sense of urgency around overcoming them. As a result, every organization in our study was investing in one (if not many) of these "strategies that win" in this increasingly complex environment.

Expanding Multichannel Strategies

All organizations in the study took advantage of a multichannel delivery system to get their offerings to the marketplace. Most were in the process of expanding these channels in search of a variety of benefits: to lure lower-potential customers to lower cost of sales channels, to meet customer demands for self-service, to expand geographic footprints, and to provide greater levels of focus to high value customers. Common channels included a field sales force, inside sales force, telemarketing unit, indirect sales force, and an e-commerce channel. Many companies were becoming increasingly focused on the use of third-party indirect sales resources (such as distributors) as a key element of the sales force, bringing questions about quality control, salesperson development, and branded customer experience. Furthermore, there was also an increasing dependence on using the service unit as a significant sales channel through the cross-sell and up-sell of inbound inquiries.

As channel options increased, channel conflict and channel misalignment was common, resulting from channels that grew as stovepipes instead of being integrated into the organization. Some organizations still struggled with how to manage customer expectations and use of channels. Most still struggled with the technological infrastructure. Overall, however, organizations were used to channel conflict and considered it a normal part of doing business. Arbitration and compensation policies were most effective in ensuring that these situations did not create inordinate inefficiencies in the organization. As organizations move forward, there is every indication that this growth in channels will continue, resulting in more formalized channel integration within regions, sales managers who act as channel managers, and salespeople who leverage other channels as an integral part of a virtual sales team.

Resegmenting and Deploying Sales Forces

We found that every organization was continuously restructuring the deployment of sales resources to maximize their return. Deployment strategies were almost always a matrixed structure based on customer characteristics, product types, sales activities, and geographies. Although inside sales was becoming more important (and more strategic in terms of sales approach), there was no indication that face-to-face sales was going away. In fact, face-to-face account management structures were common with the concept of a dedicated account rep or team being driven further and further down customer tiers. As organizations explored ways to maximize the individual talents of their sales professionals, the concept of deploying the sales force as "hunters" and "gatherers" was once again gaining favor, resulting in organizationwide assessment, evaluation, and restructuring. Even when structures stabilize, organizations must constantly reevaluate territories and revisit territory coverage. Therefore, organizations must continue to find ways in which to minimize the distraction and productivity loss from such constant restructuring.

Implementing Sales Technologies

Many organizations were looking to technology initiatives to help them leverage the size of their organization (selling as one organization, not different divisions), improve productivity (and thus increase time in the field or on the phone), and deliver consistently via multiple channels. These were difficult benefits to realize, however. In fact, almost every organization we spoke with was on their second or third generation of customer resource management (CRM) system. While some success had been achieved in using a CRM system for managerial reporting and integration of information across different parts of the organization, frontline sales representatives still did not use the systems with consistency. Although organizations were starting to invest more in the human performance side of such technologies, such initiatives continued to be technology driven rather than people or process driven.

Adopting Consultative Selling

All organizations interviewed felt that delivering on the promise of consultative selling in their markets would be a true differentiator and a key to avoiding commoditization. Consultative selling in this context meant holding needs-based conversations, assembling creative solutions from multiple products and services, displaying an unwavering focus on value, and aiming for Trusted Advisor status.

Organizations recognized that despite past efforts in this area, there was still a large gap between philosophy and execution in the field. This was due to many of the following factors: because in more prosperous times the approach may not have been worth the effort; because the philosophical approach of a consultative sale was not translated into daily processes; and because the bar for consultative selling kept rising.

To make sure that they would be more successful in their current efforts to deliver on consultative selling, organizations were devoting resources to developing sales processes and figuring out how to turn something that is a philosophy into processes and behaviors. For some organizations, this meant creating new sales processes that would help salespeople create and nurture key customer relationships—for example, building professional relationships with procurement professionals in markets that had been dominated by personal relationships. In other cases, it meant reskilling the sales force and revisiting managerial reinforcement of skills training.

Reskilling the Sales Force

Many of the organizations recognized that their current sales force would be unable to support the sales strategies being deployed. As a result, many organizations in the study had gone through vast changes in personnel (especially those that were involved in mergers). Therefore, even in a job market that favored employers, managers and directors were still very concerned over the ability to attract and retain talent that was capable of delivering on a consultative sale.

Although the skills being focused on were not new, there were now new and much higher levels of expectation in place than there had been in the past. It was no longer enough to have product knowledge, salespeople needed business acumen, industry expertise, and in-depth customer insight. They no longer needed only to be able to communicate product benefits, they needed to communicate (and even calculate) value. There was also growing interest in the idea of emotional intelligence as a precursor to sales success. Some looked at this as a selection issue (looking for salespeople with innate skills); others saw this as an awareness and development issue. Regardless of the skill set desired, obtaining it required a complete approach, starting with sales strategy and moving through assessment, performance management training, support systems, and more.

Redefining Sales Management

Organizations recognized that they were putting more demands on sales managers than they had in the past, and some were trying to find ways to better support them. Managers were now much more responsible for business decisions (à la general managers), resource management across a variety of organizations and channels, and influencing capabilities. That being said, there was still no consensus on the way to support and develop management, however. Managers were still most commonly promoted based on selling ability rather than managerial ability; development was handled by a disconnected human resources department instead of the sales training department. As a result, there is a high level of inconsistency among sales managers in the organizations (in terms of processes, decision criteria, success, etc.) and the organizations interviewed felt that there was still a lot to be done in this area.

Creating a Sales Culture

Many of the organizations we spoke with were focusing on the idea of proactively creating and maintaining a sales culture. This was usually a function of trying to integrate teams of people from different parts of a merged organization and to support frequent restructuring initiatives. Some organizations were very focused on using their culture as an important element of their brand and as a recruiting and retention tool for both sales professionals and customers.

UNDERLYING THEMES

Apart from the strategies themselves, there were other commonalties heard in our interviews—themes among the way that executives viewed their challenges and the environment in which they operated.

- *Change is constant.* There was an acceptance that change was a constant part of sales organizations. Structures would never be permanent and markets would never stabilize. Therefore, the focus was on being agile and the need to build an organization that could navigate change without being derailed with every new initiative.

- *Everything is additive.* New channels are added, but the old ones do not disappear. New customer requirements appear, but the old ones are not forgotten. As a result, there was a feeling that sales organizations will just continue to work in greater and greater complexity. Leaders were resigned to this and were concerned with which infrastructure and support systems would need to be improved to create order in this complexity.

- *The next big thing is the last big thing.* There were few ideas that were thought of as completely original—that is, not thought of before or a derivative of earlier ideas. Organizations were still talking about consultative selling. They were still trying to integrate channels and up-sell customers. Leaders, however, saw that now they were truly running out of time for philosophy without execution. There was a sense of urgency. They felt that unless they were able to really deliver on these strategies, they would suffer in the market.

- *The tougher selling environment is permanent.* There was also a common feeling that the recent economic downturn was a wake-up call that brought long-time festering issues to the forefront. Leaders were very quick to point out that these changes were permanent—that economic improvement was not going to return them to past selling environments. They were concerned that organizations would lose sight of these issues if the economy improved, and the results would be disastrous.

- *Everyone wants to be a consultant.* Building Trusted Advisor relationships with clients was viewed as the endgame for creating differentiation in the marketplace. Leaders felt that they could still, even in this demanding environment, build relationships with clients that added value. These would be hard to come by and would require higher levels of skill and knowledge, but would deliver partnerships that would move them beyond commodity status.

APPLYING THE CUSTOMER FILTER

While our survey study of small to mid-sized information technology (IT) buyers does not presume to speak for the entire world of customers, it does offer an interesting perspective on the strategies discussed in this text. The good news for sales organizations is that the customers in our survey do find a salesperson who "understands my business" to be differentiating. They are clearly more influenced by salespeople who "know the product" and are "responsive" over "friendly," and they do feel that there are more factors, such as "service reputation" and "product reputation," that can be more important than price.

On the flipside, there was little evidence that the buyers in this survey felt like their salespeople were becoming trusted business advisors. They valued their salespeople's knowledge of product features and benefits but did not look to them for "diagnosing my IT problems" or for "identifying strategic IT opportunities for me." If you think back to the Sales Impact Ladder in Chapter 5, customers in this survey characterized their salespeople as price sellers and content sellers. There is clearly, then, still a long road ahead for sales professionals. Not only will it be harder and harder to earn Trusted Advisor status with a customer, there are more and more competitors who are trying to position themselves the same way.

WHAT DO WE DO WITH ALL OF THIS INFORMATION? A FINAL THOUGHT

The clearest message that can be sent along with this book is that there is no such thing as one strategy that wins. Every organization we talked to was in the midst of undertaking several strategic initiatives to help them combat the challenges in their environment. You cannot focus on a consultative selling approach without reskilling the sales force. It would be very unlikely that you would attempt to add more channels to your sales organization without reconsidering the way you segment your sales force. And you certainly wouldn't want to restructure (e.g., into home-based offices) without considering the impact on culture. So, although we talked about each of the seven strategies in this book within its own chapter, clearly they are not distinct.

As you consider what strategies you will undertake in your own organization:

- Look at the callout boxes for ideas on best practices from some of the world's leading sales organizations, and ask yourself how recently you have focused on each of these areas. Are you proactively building a culture, or is it being created by default?

- Start with the big picture. Can you honestly say that everyone in your sales organization understands the sales strategy? Is there agreement on who you are? What you sell? Who you sell to? The value you bring? The kinds of relationships you want to create with those customers? The process for creating those relationships?

- Remember to take a holistic approach to any organizational change. Include compensation systems, performance management systems, and recruitment, selection, assessment, and training systems in your planning processes. Too often, these are misaligned with the result being sought, and when they are, tremendous amounts of resources get wasted.

- Be conscious of mindshare. Although, clearly these strategies will be implemented in tandem, the organizations in our study were careful to direct their focus on one or two key messages to the field. You cannot do everything at once. If you have to start somewhere, consider sales management. It is probably the hardest nut to crack, but it can yield the biggest rewards.

Finally, one thing that was clear in all of these organizations was the need for long-term commitment. You can't reskill a sales force over night, and establishing a culture might take years. This may seem to be common sense, but it is much more difficult than it sounds. After all, sales organizations are, more often than not, constrained by short-term tactics aimed at making short-term numbers.

Succeeding at these strategies is by no means a sure thing. It takes the insight, confidence, and commitment to make a big bet on an uncertain future. But for many, it's long past time to shake things up a bit—isn't it?

A

FIVE ROLES FOR
SUCCESSFUL SALES
A Search for the Indicators
of Sales Success

chieveGlobal conducted a series of research projects from 2000–2003 to identify what salespeople actually do and say to achieve—or undermine—their success, and the role that selling organizations play in this success or failure. The research included a review of the literature, interviews with decision makers, and the collection and analysis of more than 2,000 incidents of actual sales behaviors, both good and bad.

From this research, AchieveGlobal analyzed the work of selling—the daily observable behaviors of salespeople—and broke it down into five major roles. These roles represent the core activities of the selling process that top-performing salespeople devote the bulk of their time to and include the following:

1. Long-Term Ally
2. Business Consultant
3. Strategic Orchestrator

4. Consistent Cultivator
5. Focused Optimist

THE LONG-TERM ALLY

This role is all about the interpersonal aspect of selling and conveying a sense of shared purpose with the customer. Whether in a single 30-second phone call or a long-term relationship, successful salespeople know how to establish a human connection with customers and find opportunities to demonstrate its importance.

Star performers know how critical it is to develop mutual trust with customers. This enables them to enjoy benefits the average salesperson can only dream about, such as:

- Access to information they can leverage to keep or enhance their business
- A human connection strong enough to withstand major problems with the account, or even a new competitive product
- An identification with their products or services so strong that they become one of the "benefits" their customers will fight to keep

How do they do this? According to our research, their success is built on the following clusters of practices.

They develop client relationships. As one salesperson reported, "I was able to form a partnership with (the customer), where both of us were working together to make the product work; it wasn't just one-sided."

Another salesperson took over for someone the account didn't believe had their interests at heart. "I reestablished the account based on trust," the salesperson said, "and increased it from $65,000 to $160,000. I mended the fences and showed them I was supportive. I kept in close contact with them and monitored every aspect of their account. They needed to feel that they could trust me and feel comfortable with me."

They keep communication open. Effective salespeople find ways to communicate regularly with their customers. They know that even if there is no specific progress to report, customers appreciate knowing what is going on. Said one customer about a salesperson, "She checked in on a regular basis. I liked knowing that our account was on her mind."

About another salesperson, a respondent said, "He would research their questions and then call them back. He made regular calls on his clients even if he did not yet have an answer. He was available for them day or night. No one before had given them such service. When they needed something, they called him directly."

They become customer advocates. It's one thing to be nice to a customer. It's another to do whatever you can to make the customer look good—in the eyes of that customer's peers, boss, or own customers. "I'm always thinking, 'OK, how can I help you be successful? How can I help you be a star in your organization?'" says one very successful accounting software saleswoman. "I don't wake up in the morning saying, 'I can't wait to go out and sell something.'"

The following examples illustrate the negative behaviors that can undercut this role:

- "He was almost a caricature of a salesman—loud, jovial, overfriendly." (Buyer, transportation services)
- "My broker failed to meet with me in person to review the proposal. Communication was all via fax, e-mail, telephone, and snail mail." (Buyer, health insurance)

- "While working a trade show, I misjudged a shabbily dressed older man. I let him walk right past my booth, hoping he wouldn't stop. Wouldn't you know, he stopped at the next counter and ordered four sets for his grandchildren. That was an $8,000 loss for me." (Encyclopedia salesperson)

THE BUSINESS CONSULTANT

This role calls for salespeople who are focused, insightful, and knowledgeable about their products—as well as their customers' needs, markets, and business objectives. This knowledge enables them to serve as experts in creating solutions based on what they sell.

Star performers are such experts that they are able to completely internalize their customers' points of view. They often seem, in fact, as much employees of their customers' organizations as they are of their own. This produces the following benefits for them:

- The stature to be asked by customers to help evaluate competitors' newly-released products
- The opportunity to give advice on customers' high-level decisions and policies that have a long-term impact on future sales
- Invitations to cross-sell elsewhere in the organization (instead of having to request access)

The observable daily indicators that salespeople are performing this role include the following.

They build credible reputations. To be successful business consultants, salespeople need to be knowledgeable experts in the eyes of their customers. They need to establish their own reputations, separate from the organizations they sell for. "It's important that my customers perceive me as someone who is fully aware of their issues," said one salesperson. "Basically, if I am going to advise people, they need to believe I know what I'm talking about."

They build a solid knowledge base. Said a sales manager about one of his salesmen, "He knew his product, and he knew what he was talking about; [his knowledge] convinced the customer to give our organization the opportunity to submit a proposal." In many cases this knowledge is personal. "I personally tried (our) products, so I was aware of them all before the sale," reported a cosmetics saleswoman in China. "This made me more convincing to the customer."

Echoing the practice of many superior salespeople, one manufacturing sales rep said, "I became knowledgeable about the customer's organization. I got immersed in knowledge about them and what they wanted and needed. I had a good understanding of the company." This star performer clearly went beyond reading annual reports and prior sales figures to become familiar with the company on a cultural level.

They stay current with customers' markets and business objectives. Putting themselves in their customers' shoes by identifying market objectives is another key behavior of star performers. "I'd been trying to sell Internet advertising to a customer for eight years," said an advertising account executive. "Even though he had a Web site, he wasn't interested. During the course of last year, whenever I saw articles about ad successes in his line of business, I sent them to him. Two months ago, I made another presentation. This time he was more knowledgeable and ready to listen, and I made a very large sale." Said another salesperson, "[The customer] bought a $60,000 package because we met one of their hidden goals, which we found out by doing our research."

They develop the right solution. In today's busy world, there is no greater sales technique than demonstrating to customers that you understand their needs. As a buyer of industrial commercial hardware said, "I was thrilled that someone understood our needs and customized an approach that was tailored to my budget and my timetable." Good salespeople know that asking the right questions is key. (As one respondent said, "Selling is a process of listening to what the client wants, then educating them about exactly what they need.")

The answers to these questions enable salespeople to make sure their solutions respond to their customers' voiced and unvoiced needs. The questions don't have to be complex. As one pharmaceutical salesperson put it, "I have learned to shut up and just ask the doctors what they want. This gives me a clearly defined set of needs that I can then show how our products respond to." The truly dazzling solutions may exceed what the customer was expecting, as another respondent points out when describing this incident, "The salesman offered options that even the client didn't see; he offered an alternate equipment package and closed the sale."

They present and propose effectively. Busy customers expect salespeople to be able to present well. One salesperson of group health insurance apparently learned the importance of this skill only after an unsuccessful presentation. "As a result," she said, "this time I gathered more reliable, well-spoken, and polished team members."

Many salespeople report that they rehearse presentations before giving them. "I role-played with my managers and thought of every conceivable question they could ask me," notes one salesperson.

A well-rehearsed presentation also can forestall price objections. "Our presentation was much sharper and to the point," reported a salesperson of manufacturing machinery in South Africa. "We had every issue within the deal covered before we went in there, so we left nothing to surprise. The customer felt we knew what we were talking about and could give him the reason for the 50 percent premium on the package."

They close the sale. A successful salesperson knows when it's time to close the sale. When they see buying signals from the customer, they move to summarize benefits and ask for the order. "One reason he made such good use of his time," said a manager about a member of her sales team, "was that he knew when it was time to stop probing and asking for clarification, and wrap things up in terms of closing the sale."

Most of the negative examples in our research could have had a happy ending if the salesperson had asked—and listened—more. As it was, the salespeople in the following incidents not only missed the point, but they also gave the impression that they didn't care:

- "We did not rehearse the presentation beforehand. The organization was sloppy. Everybody did as they pleased. I should have spoken to each member (of the presentation team) ahead of time to clarify our direction." (Salesperson, group health insurance)
- "I didn't peel back the skin of the onion enough. I didn't probe deeply enough. I accepted what they said they wanted at face value." (Salesperson, training software)
- "We didn't do enough investigation of the target audience. We didn't understand their culture and environment." (Salesperson)
- "We developed a solution for a problem that didn't exist. The customers looked at us like we had three eyes." (Salesperson)
- "I ignored the fact that the customer had no technical background, and I kept talking about technical stuff. This distanced me from the customer." (Electronics salesperson, China)

- "When I was asked technical questions that I couldn't answer immediately, I said, 'I'll get back to you with answers.' The customer said, 'You don't know?' I was told to come back with someone who understands what they're talking about." (Salesperson, Japan)

THE STRATEGIC ORCHESTRATOR

Selling and buying have increasingly become team efforts. The more expensive and complex the product, the more people need to be involved on both sides of a sale. This role is all about creating connections between and within the selling and buying organizations to expedite a sale, encourage the exchange of information, and make it easy for the customer to deal with the selling organization.

The star performers of this role enjoy the following benefits that help them improve their overall sales performance:

- A network of key players in their accounts
- The ability to expedite all aspects of the selling process
- A personal infrastructure already in place within their own organizations to help them take on complex and highly profitable accounts

The observable indicators that salespeople are performing this role include the following.

They orchestrate resources to win accounts. The effective sales professional knows how to orchestrate key players in an account and in the selling organization. In some cases, these may be the technical support people. "I let their techs talk to our techs, and it keeps them happy," claims one salesperson.

In another example, a financial services salesperson worked with his initial contact to identify the decision makers in his company. "He was very grateful," said the salesperson, "because he realized he was not able to make decisions and could only take the meeting so far. By having the right people there, we were able to go quickly from an introductory meeting to making the sale."

Said one salesperson about a colleague, "This rep had a burning desire to complete a particular deal to everyone's satisfaction. On its face it seemed impossible to coordinate because of dealing with so many different people she would never see—all by fax and phone, and many with limited command of the English language. But she pulled it off."

They manage the sales process. Successful salespeople don't waste time trying to fight the customer's buying process. Instead, they look for ways to synchronize it with their own selling process. They start by doing their homework, as in this example, "I identified all the players in the client's buying process and made sure everyone in my company knew all the issues and concerns."

The most effective salespeople know how to use teamwork to succeed in today's complex buying and selling processes. One small company that sells packaging materials was able to land a large regional packaging house by involving several of its own people in the sale. "We used our president, who was instrumental in building personal rapport," said the account executive, "and a customer service person who worked exclusively with their branch operations. I took the lead in writing and giving the presentation."

A Japanese computer company that handles several hardware and software brands meets customer needs not only through its sales process, but also by involving areas of the organization, such as design, delivery, and support. "We are therefore able to provide products and services that don't compete on price. Our added value is based on ease of use and quick service, not price."

Small wonder that many salespeople report the need for project management skills. "I performed a project manager role," said one salesperson. "I set up the meetings and then provided follow-up to ensure that everything was moving smoothly. I also was the one who put the plan together in the first place, based on what I had learned in conversations with the customer."

There were several examples that illustrated process failure:

- "We are a weather-driven business and have a small window of sales opportunity. The business manager did not plan ahead to have adequate staff when the season hit. We had lots of product to deliver, but could not deliver it fast enough." (Salesperson, retail manufacturer)
- A food processor, disappointed with his distributor, asked a competing firm for a proposal. "They put one junior salesperson on it," the respondent said, "and it took her three weeks to come up with a proposal. It was good, but too late. Our existing distributor had all that time to show us that they could fix things. If the other distributor had put together a team and come up with a proposal over the weekend, they would have gotten the job." (Distribution manager, food processing company)
- A software saleswoman needed to show how her product met the needs of the heads of product development, marketing, and new business acquisition. Instead of trying to create a single purpose among all three decision makers, she pitted the needs of one person against the other— and created so much animosity that she killed the sale.

THE CONSISTENT CULTIVATOR

This role is all about the salesperson's ability to plan and manage the totality of his or her accounts. Given today's competitive pressures and the trend toward establishing long-term relationships with a few select vendors, the ability to perform this role effectively can make or break a salesperson.

Star Consistent Cultivators are in a good position to enjoy several benefits, many of them revenue related:

- Time to take on the more profitable accounts
- A reputation for reviving dormant territories or accounts
- Greater success at bringing in new accounts

The behaviors that indicate a salesperson is performing this role include the following.

They manage their time and territories. Just as a lawyer or other professional needs to know how to run a business, a salesperson needs to be able to step back and take a look at how he or she is doing relative to the organization's business objectives and his or her own goals.

The ability to be personally organized is crucial, especially if a salesperson has many small accounts. "In this industry, you don't have two or three big customers," said a salesperson for a computer equipment firm. Commenting about a colleague, he added, "He is extremely professional and exceptionally organized, and able to cover all the bases. At any time and any place you can ask him what is happening with such-and-such a customer, and he has got it at his fingertips."

Creative ways to manage personal time cropped up in several examples. Commenting on her direct supervisor, one respondent said, "We have to meet stringent sales quotas. She tripled her sales by dividing up her time. She concentrated first on the orders that were easy to fill, and did those that were harder to fill after hours, when she could concentrate."

They maintain and expand their existing accounts. Successful salespeople know where to focus their efforts. One woman who sells home furnishings had an idea to expand her business with a line of private label lamps. "She had an idea and followed all the way through with it," a respondent said. "She took the initiative to work on pricing and quantity with the stores and the manufacturer, taking on the roles of both liaison and problem solver. The result was that she made the biggest sale in the history of our company."

Although it might seem self-evident that a salesperson should target the most profitable accounts, it's not uncommon for problem accounts to swallow up most of a salesperson's time. "Sometimes," said a salesperson for health care products in Mexico City, "you find yourself dedicating most of your time to your most difficult clients, and forgetting about the rest because they seem secure. You then lose contact with them and forget their needs. Then someone else can come in."

An excellent way to solidify and expand your base is to have measurable evidence of your product's success in an account. "With 15 years of relations with the customer, it was very easy to document our standing with end users in the firm," said a salesperson of commercial printing services. "When a new manager threatened to take their business somewhere else, we were able to present testimonials, samples of work, and a short pricing structure to show him in quantifiable terms what he was getting. He ended up staying with us."

Some salespeople are able to prosper by selling broadly and deeply into existing accounts. Others depend more on leads. One group of salespeople in an office services company had to get creative when a traditional source of leads dried up. "We dreamed up a contest to get referrals from local merchants," the respondent said. "We set a goal of getting three referrals from each source, and it paid off."

The following examples illustrate the negative behaviors that can undercut this role:

- "Once the vendor had our business, they ignored us, never visited. No communication, not even by e-mail. Winning a bid is just the beginning of a long-term relationship. You have to feed it, maintain it." (Buyer of computer equipment)

- "We were going for a big contract. We did all the right things except that we bypassed one department. That one manager was able to get the contract canceled. And he bad-mouthed us throughout the region." (Account executive)

- "We haven't really put a metric in place to determine the best clients to work with. We use a 'this client just feels right for us' approach. So I have a lot of proposals without any direction or boundaries. That's me: too many irons in the fire, too many things going on with 'potential,' no way of prioritizing." (Salesperson/account manager)

- "We accepted an invitation to submit a proposal and spent more than $50,000 on it without knowing very much about the client. It was based on the false feeling that we needed the work. Needless to say, we didn't get it. Later on, we realized we wouldn't have wanted it." (Salesperson, construction and engineering firm)

- "Nobody in the company was focused on goals. They were performing 'the illusion of work'—and waiting for customers to call them." (Insurance salesperson)

THE FOCUSED OPTIMIST

The more competitive, challenging, and difficult the selling environment becomes, the more critical it is for salespeople to retain the ability to keep moving forward. This role is all about what top performers do to create a positive atmosphere that makes selling an enjoyable and frequent activity for sellers and buyers alike.

Their secret seems to be a combination of never-give-up persistence and an ability to maintain a sense of optimism that keeps them moving forward and causes others to want to work with them. The star performers of this role enjoy several payoffs:

- The energy to persevere during tough times
- Access to the hard-to-reach top decision makers in their accounts
- Consistently returned phone calls from customers

The behaviors that indicate a salesperson is able to maintain an optimistic outlook include the following.

They are motivated to succeed. The most successful salespeople seem to love what they're doing, and it shows. Said one, "Selling gives you pleasure. I couldn't describe it. It not only fills your pocket, but also your spirit and your heart." What's more, this attitude is infectious, as a salesman for security equipment noted about one of his colleagues, "This person exuded confidence. Customers sensed the joy he felt in what he was doing and the confidence that he had."

Enthusiasm can sometimes make up for lack of experience. "A brand-new consultant in my unit, with very little training, sold over $400 on her very first appointment," said a cosmetics saleswoman. "She was so excited about the product that everyone who attended (the session) believed her enough to make a purchase!"

Another novice, selling security equipment, did her homework but also used her enthusiasm and lack of experience to land the biggest sale in her group. As a colleague noted, "She was so enthusiastic and eager, and formed a good relationship with the customer because they were eager to help her out. She made 150 percent of her quota."

About a copy machine salesman who made a sale at the last possible moment, a colleague said, "He had a belief in his own product that rubbed off on the customer. He was determined not to let this sale go—even though he knew the customer had already made her decision."

A few salespeople in our research fueled their optimism with the doubts expressed by other people. As a salesperson for an alarm systems company put it, "People were against me; they told me it couldn't be done, I could never make the sale. I just wanted to prove to them that they were talking nonsense. And I did."

They meet their commitments. One way of demonstrating a positive attitude is by meeting—and exceeding—your commitments. "I have always been able to deliver what I promise," said an enthusiastic salesman, "and (the account) appreciates it. Because of this, I was able to sign them to a $300,000 contract."

"I don't mind rolling up my sleeves and going to work," said a salesman of heavy manufacturing machinery. "If the customer is really busy, I might jump on a forklift and help out."

They get and keep the customer's attention. Optimism helps, but without persistence it serves no purpose. Persistence, in fact, was one of the most frequently mentioned qualities of top performers.

According to the research, top performers are not afraid to be creative to get their foot in the door, as in this example: "The salesperson had a great idea of sending a coconut with a note painted on the outside. The customer laughed and called to find out who had sent such a crazy thing."

A representative for a greeting card company in France described five years of effort just to land a meeting. "I kept calling the store owner," he said, "and sending him my cards, and eventually I succeeded in getting the meeting."

There's a fine line, however, between being persistent and being a pest. One salesperson said, "I always feel that you should be in a client's face, so that when they need you, they remember you." It would be interesting to know how his clients view this behavior.

The following examples illustrate the negative behaviors that can undercut this role:

- Persistence combined with a lack of preparedness is a recipe for failure, as in this incident: "If the salesperson had spent more time learning about our company and less time badgering people for a meeting, he would have done better." (Buyer of office products)
- "We maybe had a chance for the sale. However, I didn't feel like giving up my weekend for a maybe." (Salesperson)
- "He got 'busy' and buzzed off a client too many times." (Store manager)
- "I got too proud of my excellent results in the first half, so I didn't work hard the second half. I even went home for naps during business hours. Because I wasn't trying to get new customers, I had to rely on my existing customers for referrals. My sales results plunged." (Car salesperson, Tokyo)
- "Instead of letting them know we could get it within the hour, the salesperson just told them we didn't have it." (Sales manager)
- "She spends too much time complaining about her problems. People don't like to be around that for too long. It's heavy." (Sales manager)

SUPPORTING THE SELLING PROCESS: WHAT ORGANIZATIONS CAN DO

The job of selling comes with a unique set of challenges. Salespeople are out there every day—risking rejection to advance their organization, struggling to outsell the competition, trying to identify and stay on top of new opportunities, and making time to enhance relations with existing customers.

It's true that many salespeople are self-motivated. Even the most motivated, however, benefit from organizational support—and can suffer when it's missing. It is this support that can move average performers into the top ranks and help top players polish their star.

What types of support do they want? Here is what some salespeople in our research had to say.

- *Focus.* "I have so much going on, I can easily get distracted. I use the compensation plan to focus. . . . It's hard to stay focused on abstract concepts like a 'business plan.' So if our comp plan rewards new business, that's what I'll go out and get." (Salesperson)
- *Information.* "One way the organization distracts me is by not giving me the information I need. Last week, nobody could give me some pricing I desperately needed . . . so I made it up. This is time consuming and very stressful." (Salesperson)
- *Useful tools.* "I use a time-management software program that lets me track customers, keep to-do lists, everything. The ironic thing is I battled the company for years to let me use it. Now it's the company standard." (Salesperson)

RESEARCH METHODOLOGY

The study consisted of one-on-one interviews, surveys, and reviews of "critical incidences." A total of 33 interviews were conducted from February to April, 2000, 24 with people in the United States and 9 with people from Italy, Switzerland, and Great Britain. The study focused on organizations ranging in size from 100 employees to more than 10,000 employees. They represented all business sectors, including heavy manufacturing, high-tech manufacturing, financial services, health and social services, business services, retail and distribution, transportation and utilities, government, and education.

More than 470 people responded to the survey. Participants in this part of the study were sales managers or salespeople, usually identified by a key contact within each organization. These responses generated more than 2,100 critical incidences. These were entered into a database along with information identifying participant characteristics. As a result of the analysis, these incidences were aggregated into a set of 16 selling competencies, and then further divided into the 5 key roles of effective salespeople.

B

SALESPERSON
COMPETENCY ASSESSMENT

The following questionnaire is designed to help you assess this person's sales skills and abilities. Please answer each question by circling the number that best represents your response. For each question, indicate the extent to which this person *actually uses the skill* described in the statement. Please keep in mind the following:

- N means "Not applicable"
- 1 means "Not at all"
- 4 means "To some extent"
- 7 means "To a very great extent"

Please feel free to use numbers between those described to accurately indicate the level of skill use. If a skill does not apply to your organization, circle N. The questionnaire is divided into 16 sections. In each section, look through the items and select the one where you feel this person needs to improve the most. For this item, place an "X" in the column marked "Area Needing the Most Improvement."

EXAMPLE

Area Needing the Most Improvement
(Choose 1 per section)

	Not at All		To Some Extent		To a Very Great Extent	

To what extent does this person ...

1. Focus on client's long-term
   interests?   N   1 │ 2   3   4 │⑤ 6   7 │ ☒

In this example, the answer indicates that, in your opinion, the extent to which this person focuses on client's long-term interests is between "To some extent" and "To a very great extent." Furthermore, you feel that focusing on clients' long-term interests is the area in which this person needs the most improvement.

As you answer each item:

- Think about the behavior and attitudes of this person. It might help to reflect on specific experiences.
- Give your first impression when answering. Don't spend a lot of time on any one item.
- Be frank. Your responses are completely confidential. We want your candid response to each of these questions.

Please answer the following questions keeping this person's skills and abilities in mind.

	Not at All					To Some Extent			To a Very Great Extent	

Long-Term Ally
To what extent does this person . . .

A. Develop Client Relationship

1. Demonstrate consideration for the client? N 1 2 3 4 5 6 7 ☐

2. Develop solid relationship with the client? N 1 2 3 4 5 6 7 ☐

3. Adapt sales approach to each client? N 1 2 3 4 5 6 7 ☐

4. Focus on client's long-term interests? N 1 2 3 4 5 6 7 ☐

B. Keep Communications Open

5. Maintain the relationship after the sale? N 1 2 3 4 5 6 7 ☐

6. Provide a continuing high level of commitment? N 1 2 3 4 5 6 7 ☐

7. Initiate regular contact with client? N 1 2 3 4 5 6 7 ☐

8. Actively listen to what the client says? N 1 2 3 4 5 6 7 ☐

C. Become the Customer's Advocate

9. Demonstrate personal commitment to the client? N 1 2 3 4 5 6 7 ☐

10. Make an extra effort to meet a client need? N 1 2 3 4 5 6 7 ☐

11. Correct mistakes made by others? N 1 2 3 4 5 6 7 ☐

Strategic Orchestrator

D. Orchestrate Resources to Win the Account

12. Bring in the right people to win the account? N 1 2 3 4 5 6 7 ☐

13. Interact well with client's key players? N 1 2 3 4 5 6 7 ☐

Please answer the following questions keeping this person's skills and abilities in mind.

Area Needing the Most Improvement
(Choose 1 per section)

	Not at All		To Some Extent			To a Very Great Extent			

E. Manage the Sales Process

14. Coordinate the resources needed to support the sales effort?   N 1 | 2 3 4 | 5 6 7 | ☐

15. Build the right team to support the client?   N 1 | 2 3 4 | 5 6 7 | ☐

Focused Optimist

F. Motivated to Succeed

16. Show enthusiasm for products and services?   N 1 | 2 3 4 | 5 6 7 | ☐

17. Make frequent contact with a potential customer?   N 1 | 2 3 4 | 5 6 7 | ☐

18. Overcome obstacles to achieve goals?   N 1 | 2 3 4 | 5 6 7 | ☐

G. Get and Keep Client's Attention

19. Get the client's attention?   N 1 | 2 3 4 | 5 6 7 | ☐

20. Get appointments with the right decision makers?   N 1 | 2 3 4 | 5 6 7 | ☐

H. Meet Commitments

21. Submit bids or proposals on time?   N 1 | 2 3 4 | 5 6 7 | ☐

22. Respond to client promptly?   N 1 | 2 3 4 | 5 6 7 | ☐

23. Follow up to ensure on-time delivery of products and services?   N 1 | 2 3 4 | 5 6 7 | ☐

Consistent Cultivator

I. Manage Time and Territory

24. Focus on developing new accounts?   N 1 | 2 3 4 | 5 6 7 | ☐

25. Use well-thought-out criteria to qualify prospects?   N 1 | 2 3 4 | 5 6 7 | ☐

26. Focus on the most profitable clients?   N 1 | 2 3 4 | 5 6 7 | ☐

Please answer the following questions keeping this person's skills and abilities in mind.	Not at All		To Some Extent			To a Very Great Extent			*Area Needing the Most Improvement* **(Choose 1 per section)**
27. Devote resources to winnable accounts?	N	1	2	3	4	5	6	7	☐
28. Prospect new accounts?	N	1	2	3	4	5	6	7	☐

J. Maintain and Expand Accounts

29. Identify new opportunities in an account?	N	1	2	3	4	5	6	7	☐
30. Evaluate client satisfaction with the product or service?	N	1	2	3	4	5	6	7	☐
31. Provide useful information to clients on an ongoing basis?	N	1	2	3	4	5	6	7	☐
32. Identify future issues and needs?	N	1	2	3	4	5	6	7	☐

Business Consultant

K. Build a Credible Reputation

33. Use organization's reputation to get additional business?	N	1	2	3	4	5	6	7	☐
34. Inspire credibility in products and services?	N	1	2	3	4	5	6	7	☐
35. Demonstrate knowledge to build credibility?	N	1	2	3	4	5	6	7	☐

L. Build a Solid Knowledge Base

36. Understand the organization's products and services?	N	1	2	3	4	5	6	7	☐
37. Gather information about competitors?	N	1	2	3	4	5	6	7	☐

M. Stay Current with Customer Markets and Business Objectives

38. Gather information about the client's organization?	N	1	2	3	4	5	6	7	☐
39. Gather information about the client's industry and marketplace?	N	1	2	3	4	5	6	7	☐
40. Understand client's decision-making process?	N	1	2	3	4	5	6	7	☐

Please answer the following questions keeping this person's skills and abilities in mind.

	Not at All		To Some Extent			To a Very Great Extent			

N. Develop the Right Solution

41. Understand client's needs thoroughly? N 1 2 3 4 5 6 7 ☐

42. Develop solutions to meet client's needs? N 1 2 3 4 5 6 7 ☐

43. Ask questions to uncover client's needs? N 1 2 3 4 5 6 7 ☐

O. Present and Propose Effectively

44. Write compelling proposals? N 1 2 3 4 5 6 7 ☐

45. Take time to prepare for sales calls and presentations? N 1 2 3 4 5 6 7 ☐

46. Present well to clients? N 1 2 3 4 5 6 7 ☐

47. Focus on value of products and services? N 1 2 3 4 5 6 7 ☐

48. Provide samples or demonstrations of capabilities? N 1 2 3 4 5 6 7 ☐

P. Close the Sale

49. Overcome client objections? N 1 2 3 4 5 6 7 ☐

50. Highlight product or service advantages over competitors? N 1 2 3 4 5 6 7 ☐

51. Ask for the sale? N 1 2 3 4 5 6 7 ☐

52. Negotiate an agreement that satisfies all parties? N 1 2 3 4 5 6 7 ☐

53. Convince the client of the value of the products or services? N 1 2 3 4 5 6 7 ☐

C

SALES MANAGER ASSESSMENT

The following questionnaire is designed to help you assess this person's sales leadership. Please answer each question by circling the number that best represents your response. For each question, indicate the extent to which this person *actually uses the skill* described in the statement. Please keep in mind the following:

- N means "Not applicable"
- 1 means "Not at all"
- 4 means "To some extent"
- 7 means "To a very great extent"

Please feel free to use numbers between those described to accurately indicate the level of skill use. If a skill does not apply to your organization, circle N.

The questionnaire is divided into six sections. In each section, look through the items and select the one where you feel this person needs to improve the most. For this item, place an "X" in the column marked "Area Needing the Most Improvement."

EXAMPLE

Area Needing the Most Improvement
(Choose 1 per section)

	Not at All	To Some Extent	To a Very Great Extent	

To what extent does this person . . .

1. Observe sales calls, model sales skills, and provide one-on-one coaching? N 1 | 2 3 4 |(5) 6 7 |X

In this example, the answer indicates that, in your opinion, the extent to which this person observes sales calls, models sales skills, and provides one-on-one coaching is between "To some extent" and "To a very great extent." Furthermore, you feel that observing sales calls, modeling sales skills, and providing one-on-one coaching is the area in which this person needs the most improvement.

As you answer each item:

- Think about the behavior and attitudes of this person. It might help to reflect on specific experiences.
- Give your first impression when answering. Don't spend a lot of time on any one item.
- Be frank. Your responses are completely confidential. We want your candid responses to each of these questions.

Please answer the following questions keeping this person's skills and abilities in mind.

Area Needing the Most Improvement
(Choose 1 per section)

	Not at All		To Some Extent		To a Very Great Extent			

COACH ROLE
To what extent does this person . . .

A. Build a Cohesive Team

1. Resolve conflict within the team?   N   1 | 2   3   4 | 5   6   7   ☐

2. Promote team spirit and cohesiveness among all staff members?   N   1 | 2   3   4 | 5   6   7   ☐

3. Treat all members of the sales team fairly and equitably, regardless of personal relationships or personalities?   N   1 | 2   3   4 | 5   6   7   ☐

4. Delegate decision making to the team whenever possible?   N   1 | 2   3   4 | 5   6   7   ☐

B. Develop Professional Skills of Individuals in the Sales Organization

5. Provide sales support and guidance as needed?   N   1 | 2   3   4 | 5   6   7   ☐

6. Provide appropriate training to build salespeople's skills and knowledge?   N   1 | 2   3   4 | 5   6   7   ☐

7. Observe sales calls, model sales skills, and provide one-on-one coaching?   N   1 | 2   3   4 | 5   6   7   ☐

8. Review salespeople's performance on a regular basis?   N   1 | 2   3   4 | 5   6   7   ☐

C. Motivate Individuals in the Sales Organization

9. Give salespeople authority to make decisions regarding their sales activities?   N   1 | 2   3   4 | 5   6   7   ☐

10. Set high but attainable standards and expectations?   N   1 | 2   3   4 | 5   6   7   ☐

11. Use incentives and other strategies to help salespeople stay motivated?   N   1 | 2   3   4 | 5   6   7   ☐

12. Give recognition for individual efforts?   N   1 | 2   3   4 | 5   6   7   ☐

Please answer the following questions keeping this person's skills and abilities in mind.

Area Needing the Most Improvement
(Choose 1 per section)

	Not at All		To Some Extent			To a Very Great Extent			

D. Assist in Sales Call Activities

13. Step in to resolve problems with clients?   N 1 2 3 4 5 6 7 ☐

14. Identify and talk with prospects when necessary?   N 1 2 3 4 5 6 7 ☐

15. Provide guidance in qualifying opportunities?   N 1 2 3 4 5 6 7 ☐

16. Work with the sales force to strategize accounts?   N 1 2 3 4 5 6 7 ☐

STRATEGIST ROLE
To what extent does this person ...

E. Create, Communicate, and Execute a Vision for Your Sales Organization

17. Make decisions and develop team policies that further the organization's objectives?   N 1 2 3 4 5 6 7 ☐

18. Develop and communicate a mission and vision for the sales team?   N 1 2 3 4 5 6 7 ☐

19. Ensure that the sales team adheres to company policies?   N 1 2 3 4 5 6 7 ☐

F. Develop an Approach to the Marketplace

20. Analyze the marketplace (sizing, segmentation, trends, etc.)?   N 1 2 3 4 5 6 7 ☐

21. Develop and execute business development initiatives (ads, promotions, etc.)?   N 1 2 3 4 5 6 7 ☐

G. Manage Resources Effectively

22. Secure resources from the organization necessary to support sales (staff or support from other departments, financial resources, software, equipment, etc.)?   N 1 2 3 4 5 6 7 ☐

Please answer the following questions keeping this person's skills and abilities in mind.

	Not at All		To Some Extent		To a Very Great Extent				

23. Evaluate and manage staff based on performance data? — N 1 2 3 4 5 6 7 ☐

24. Review and manage budgets/ expenses as well as profitability? — N 1 2 3 4 5 6 7 ☐

25. Manage distribution channels and their impact on the field? — N 1 2 3 4 5 6 7 ☐

26. Select/recruit talented salespeople to meet client demand? — N 1 2 3 4 5 6 7 ☐

H. Maintain Current Knowledge Base

27. Keep product knowledge current? — N 1 2 3 4 5 6 7 ☐

28. Understand marketplace, competitive environment, competitive products, and points of differentiation? — N 1 2 3 4 5 6 7 ☐

COMMUNICATOR ROLE
To what extent does this person . . .

I. Communicate Effectively to Other Parts of the Organization

29. Represent the field's view to upper management? — N 1 2 3 4 5 6 7 ☐

30. Keep superiors informed of the sales team's progress? — N 1 2 3 4 5 6 7 ☐

31. Maintain good working relationships with other departments? — N 1 2 3 4 5 6 7 ☐

J. Communicate Information from Other Parts of the Organization to Sales Staff

32. Keep sales team informed on changes that are going on in the organization? — N 1 2 3 4 5 6 7 ☐

33. Communicate corporate strategies to the sales team? — N 1 2 3 4 5 6 7 ☐

Please answer the following questions keeping this person's skills and abilities in mind.

Area Needing the Most Improvement
(Choose 1 per section)

	Not at All		To Some Extent			To a Very Great Extent			

K. Solicit and Value Feedback from the Sales Team

34. Actively encourage salespeople to express opinions?

    N   1 | 2   3   4 | 5   6   7   ☐

35. Create or reevaluate policies/make decisions based on team's input?

    N   1 | 2   3   4 | 5   6   7   ☐

L. Facilitate Information Sharing among Sales Staff

36. Provide mechanism (e-mail, meetings, conference calls, intranet, newsletter, etc.) for information sharing among the team?

    N   1 | 2   3   4 | 5   6   7   ☐

37. Create culture/atmosphere where information sharing is promoted?

    N   1 | 2   3   4 | 5   6   7   ☐

Abele, John, William Caesar, and Roland H. John. 2003. "Rechanneling Sales." *McKinsey Quarterly* 3.

Aksin, O. Z. and Harker, P. T. 1999. "To Sell or Not to Sell: Determining the Trade-offs between Service and Sales in Retail Banking Phone Centers." *Journal of Service Research* 2, no. 1 (August): 19–33.

Behrman, Douglas N., and William D. Perreault Jr. 1984. "A Role Stress Model of the Performance and Satisfaction of Industrial Salespersons." *Journal of Marketing* 48 (Fall): 9–21.

Beverland, Michael. 2001. "Contextual Influence and the Adoption and Practice of Relationship Selling in a Business-to-Business Setting: An Exploratory Study." *Journal of Personal Selling and Sales Management* 21, no. 3 (Summer): 207–215.

Brendler, William F. 2001. "8 Critical Factors That Make or Break CRM." *Target Marketing* (April): 57–61.

Brennan, Michael. 2004. "Flying in Formation: The Organization Commitment of Training and Development." *CLO Magazine* (March): 50–52.

Churchill, Gilbert A. Jr., Neil M. Ford, and Orville C. Walker Jr. 1990. *Sales Force Management*, 3rd ed. Homewood: Richard D. Irwin.

Cichelli, David J. 2003. "2004 Sales Compensation Trends Survey." Executive Summary, The Alexander Group, Inc., 2.

Compton, Jason. 2004. "Despite Billions in CRM Investment, Financial Customers Still Ready to Walk." *Destination CRM* e-newsletter, April 6, 2004.

Costello, D. 2000. "New Measures of CRM Performance." Customer Relationship Management 2000, (October), 49–62.

CRMCommunity.com. Homepage viewed December 29, 2003.

Del Gaizo, Edward. 1989. "Building a Curriculum That Works." *Personnel* (November): 58–61.

————. "Creating Sales Superstars." 2001. AchieveGlobal white paper.

DePree, Max. 2004. *Leadership Is an Art.* New York: Doubleday.

Dickie, Jim, and Barry Trailer. 2004. "Sales Effective Insights—The Top Ten Trends for 2004." *CSO Insights.*

Dubinsky, Alan J. et al. 1996. "Salesforce Socialization." *Journal of Marketing* 50–54, 192–208.

————. 1996. "Some Assumptions about the Effectiveness of Sales Training." *Journal of Personal Selling and Sales Management* (Summer): 67–76.

Equation Research. 2002. "Prisoners of Paperwork." *Sales and Marketing Management.* (December) 41–45.

Forrester Research, Inc. 2003. *Optimism toward eCommerce Returns.* (December 30).

Futrell, Charles, and A. Parasuraman. 1984. "The Relationship of Satisfaction and Performance to Salesforce Turnover." *Journal of Marketing* 48 (Fall): 33–46.

Galea, Christine. 2002. "2002 Annual Training Survey." *Sales and Marketing Magazine* (July): 34–37.

Goleman, Daniel. 1995. *Emotional Intelligence: Why It Can Matter More Than IQ.* New York: Bantam Books.

Gschwandtner, G. 2001. "The CRM Promise vs. Reality." *Selling Power* (April).

Ingram, Thomas N. et al. 2002. "Selling in the New Millennium, a Joint Agenda." *Industrial Marketing Management,* no. 31: 559–67.

Jackson, Donald W. Jr., Stephen S. Tax, and John W. Barnes. 1994. "Examining the Sales Force Culture: Managerial Applications and Research Propositions." *Journal of Professional Selling and Sales Management* 14, no. 4 (Fall).

Keilor, Bruce et al. 2000. "Relationship-Oriented Characteristics and Individual Salesperson Performance." *Journal of Business and Industrial Marketing* 22, no. 1: 7–22.

Kohli, Ajay K. 1985. "Some Unexplored Supervisory Behaviors and Their Influence on Salespeople's Role Clarity, Specific Self-Esteem, Job Satisfaction, and Motivation." *Journal of Marketing Research* 22 (November): 424–433.

Krishnamurthy, Chandru et al. 2003. "Solutions Selling: Is the Pain Worth the Gain?" McKinsey Marketing Solutions white paper. (April)

Ligos, Melinda ed. 2002. "Highlights from our Chief Sales Executive Forum." *Sales & Marketing Management* (November).

Malo, Keith, and Mark Marone. 2002. "Technology in the Sales Organization." *Selling Power* (April).

Mayer, J.D. and P. Salovey. 1993. "The Intelligence of Emotional Intelligence." *Intelligence,* 17(4), 433–42.

Mehta, Rajiv, Bert Rosenbloom, and Rolph Anderson. 2000. "Role of the Sales Manager in Channel Management: Impact of Organizational Variables." *Journal of Personal Selling and Sales Management* 20, no. 2 (Spring): 81–88.

Mirani, R., D. Moore, and J. A. Weber. 2001. "Emerging Technologies for Enhancing Supplier-Reseller Partnerships." *Industrial Marketing Management* 30: 101–114.

Mobley, William. 1982. *Employee Turnover Causes Consequences and Control.* Reading: Addison-Wesley.

Mowday, R. T., R. M. Steers, and L. W. Porter. 1979. "The Measurement of Organizational Commitments." *Journal of Vocational Behavior* 14: 224–247.

Nunes, Paul, and Frank Cespedes. 2003. "The Customer Has Escaped." *Harvard Business Review* (November).

Ott, Steven. 1989. *The Organizational Culture Perspective.* Chicago: Dorsey Press.

Randall, James E. and Cindy H. Randall. 2001. "A Current Review of Hiring Techniques for Sales Personnel: The First Step in the Sales Management Process." *Journal of Marketing Theory and Practice* (Spring): 70–83.

Schaaf, Jeanne. 2004. "SMB Benchmark Survey." Unpublished research report.

Schein, Edgar H. 1984. *Organizational Culture and Leadership.* San Francisco: Jossey-Bass.

Schillewaert, Niels, and Michael Ahearne. 2003. "A Survey of More Than 1,000 Sales Execs and Reps Find That Users Need Better Training and Support, Not Top-Flight Technology." *Destination CRM* (Dec. 1). Penn State. <http://www.destinationcrm.com>.

Thompson, B. 2001. "What Is CRM?" *Customer Relationship Management Primer 2001* (January): 1–3.

———. 2003. "Keeping Customers Is Smart and Profitable. *Business Week* (July 3).

Watson Wyatt Worldwide. 2002. "Sales Force Compensation and Management: Driving the Top Line in Changing Times." Self-published research report.

William, Powell. 2001. "Train Today, Sell Tomorrow." *Training and Development Journal* (September): 43.

Wilson, Phillip H. et al. 2002. "Investigating the Perceptual Aspect of Sales Training." *The Journal of Personal Selling & Sales Management* 22, no. 2 (Spring): 77–86.

Zoltners, Andris A., Prabhakant Sinha, Greggor A. Zoltners. 2001. *The Complete Guide to Accelerating Sales Force Performance.* Amacom, New York.